"All too often Ch
ed on a vital faith in
do it. *The Journey of*
stand what faith in Christ really is; and in a very practical, exciting way they will come to understand how to live their faith in Christ every day. All churches should take this journey together! *The Journey of Faith* is a must for pastors, missionaries, teachers and all church members!"

        Ernest McAninch
        LifeWay Christian Resources

"*The Journey of Faith*, written by an outstanding pastor and wife who know full well what this journey is all about, is an excellent guide to aid in beginning the vital journey toward living the faith-filled life. An interesting and inspirational writing style makes this an important instrument for any who have a desire to "walk by faith and not by sight." This is a practical discipleship study guide appropriate for use by an individual, a family unit, small groups, or Bible Study groups. Anyone who sincerely wants to live a life filled with faith should use this book."

        Dr. Levi Price
        Truett Theological Seminary

"Rob Boyd is a gifted communicator. In *The Journey of Faith*, you will be challenged to go where few have been with God. You will also have the opportunity to walk with one who smiles broadly with pleasure as we learn new ways to walk in faith."

        Dr. Thane Barnes
        Executive Director
        Nevada Baptist Convention

"The life that pleases God is a life of faith in Him. This book biblically, practically, and powerfully teaches us how to live by faith and thus please God. You will be blessed."

                      Dr. Fred Wolfe, Former Pastor
                      Cottage Hill Baptist Church
                      Mobile, AL

"Faith is the key that unlocks the immeasurable resources of God for the believer. If we fail to use that key, we can't please God. Rob Boyd is a dear friend and passionate follower of the Lord Jesus Christ. I can't think of a better person to open up for us the riches of Hebrews 11 and hand us the key of faith. I am looking forward to getting my hands on this powerful devotional book!"

                      Dr. Chuck Herring, Pastor
                      First Baptist Church
                      Collierville, TN

"Rob and Lisa have produced a book that is biblical, practical, inspirational, and quite frankly, POWERFUL! It is a unique combination of humor and life experiences, encapsulated with biblical truths that can absolutely transform your life!"

                      Dr. Hal Kitchings, Pastor
                      First Baptist Church
                      Eustis, FL

"Rob Boyd has always been one of my favorite preachers. Now he and his wife Lisa have become two of my favorite writers. Everything about *The Journey of Faith* is practical, challenging, and relevant. You are in for a rewarding experience with God."

                      Dr. Gary Permenter
                      Gary Permenter Ministries

THE JOURNEY OF FAITH

A 40-Day Spiritual Experience
Through Hebrews 11

Rob and Lisa Boyd

www.CrossHousePublishing.org

To order more copies
of *The Journey of Faith*
and related products
Contact: Green Valley Baptist Church
270 N. Valle Verde Dr.
Henderson, NV 89074
www.greenvalleybc.org
CALL: 1-702-434-1906

Copyright Rob and Lisa Boyd, 2006
All Rights Reserved
Printed in the United States of America
Cover design by Greg Crull

All Scripture quotations, unless otherwise indicated, are taken from the *Holy Bible, New International Version.* "NIV". Copyright 1973, 1978, 1984 by International Bible Society. Used by permission of Zondervan. All rights reserved.

Scripture quotations marked MSG are from THE MESSAGE. Copyright by Eugene H. Peterson 1993, 1994, 1995, 1996, 2000, 2001, 2002. Used by permission of NavPress Publishing Group.

Scripture quotations marked AB are from *The Amplified Bible.* Old Testament Copyright 1965, 1987, by the Zondervan Corporation. Used by permission. All rights reserved. New Testament Copyright 1954, 1958, 1987, by The Lockman Foundation. Used by permission.

Scripture quotations marked "NKJV" are taken from the New King James Version. Copyright 1982 by Thomas Nelson, Inc. Used by permission. All rights reserved.

Scripture quotations marked (NLT) are taken from the *Holy Bible, New Living Translation,* copyright 1996. Used by permission of Tyndale House Publishers, Inc., Wheaton, IL 60189 USA. All rights reserved.

*This book is dedicated to Green Valley Baptist Church.
Words cannot express how much you mean to us.
You are the answer to a dream
God placed deep within our hearts.
We consider it an honor to serve God alongside you.*

CONTENTS

Introduction	8
1. What Is Faith?	12
2. How to Please God	17
3. The Power of God	22
4. What It Means to Worship	27
5. Walking with God	32
6. God-Pleasing Faith	36
7. Faith That Obeys God	41
8. The Step of Faith	47
9. Faith in God's Promises	52
10. Citizens of Heaven	58
11. When Your Faith Waivers	64
12. The Blessings of God	70
13. Strangers on Earth	76
14. What Makes You Different?	81
15. Never Look Back	87
16. Assurance of Salvation	92
17. The Testing of Our Faith	97
18. When God Doesn't Make Sense	103
19. Miracles and Faith	109
20. How to Bless Your Children	115
21. An Encounter with God	121
22. When Good Comes from Bad	126
23. Making Decisions by Faith	132
24. Humility	137
25. Choosing to Live for God	143
26. When Persecution Comes	148
27. The Fear of God	153

28. Power in the Blood	159
29. God's Protection	164
30. Your Way or God's Way	169
31. Can God Use You?	175
32. Modern-Day Idols	180
33. The Power of the Holy Spirit	186
34. Ordinary People	192
35. Praying in Faith	199
36. The Sovereignty of God	205
37. The Arrows of Affliction	211
38. Turning Tragedy into Worship	217
39. Delayed Rewards	222
40. Perfect People in a Perfect Place	228
Conclusion	*235*
Endnotes	*236*

INTRODUCTION

In a poverty-stricken village on the island of Jamaica, I began my journey of faith. It wasn't anything I planned, but God orchestrated my life to the point where I had to choose the path I would follow in life. I had to decide whether I would walk by fact or by faith.

Walking by fact was familiar and comfortable, and I was confident of moderate success. It was the only road I knew. I had carefully planned out my future. I majored in accounting, which I considered a very sensible choice. After graduation, I took a job at a CPA firm. My future looked bright to the outside world, yet inside I sensed something was missing.

Unexpectedly, I was invited to go on a mission trip to Jamaica. At that time in my life I had never flown on an airplane or traveled outside of the United States. The purpose of the trip was ministry-oriented, but all I could think about was a Caribbean vacation. Although I went for all the wrong reasons, God knew exactly why I was going to Jamaica.

When we arrived in Jamaica, five of us piled into a small sedan and traveled to a remote village. It was nowhere near the beach. For seven days we lived in the most miserable conditions I had ever experienced. There was no running water, no air conditioning, and very little electricity. I didn't shower for days and the little food we had did not sit well in my stomach. The living conditions of these people were deplorable. I could not imagine living in such a place.

By the end of the fourth day, I was ready to go home. I was miserable, frustrated, and angry. God had ruined my tropical vacation! I decided to walk through the village by myself. I stopped and spoke with the local residents, and as I got to know them, I was startled at what I learned. These people had no material possessions, and yet they seemed content. Although I had more "things" than anyone in the village, I was the unhappiest person in town.

At that moment, God spoke to me on a dirt road in Jamaica and reminded me of His words in Matthew 6:19-21.

> Do not store up for yourselves treasures on earth, where moth and rust destroy, and where thieves break in and steal. But store up for yourselves treasures in heaven, where moth and rust do not destroy, and where thieves do not break in and steal. For where your treasure is, there your heart will be also.

On that dusty road in Jamaica, I chose to start walking by faith and not by fact. I did not know where my journey of faith would lead, but I believed with all of my heart that it was the will of God for my life.

Two decades have passed since that pivotal day in Jamaica. It has been exciting, frightening, challenging, and difficult at times…but never boring. The best way I can describe my journey of faith is through a poem I received from a teenager named Valerie many years ago.

"The Road of Life"

> At first I saw God as my observer, my judge, keeping track of the things I did wrong, so as to know whether I merited heaven or hell when I die. He was sort of like our president in a way. I recognized his picture but I didn't really know him.
>
> But later on, when I met Christ, it seemed as though life were rather like a bike ride. But it was a tandem bike, and I noticed that Christ was in the back helping me pedal.

I don't know just when it was that he suggested we change places, but life has not been the same since.

When I was in control, I knew the way. It was rather boring and predictable. It was the shortest distance between two points. But when he took the lead, he knew delightful long cuts up the mountains and through rocky places at breakneck speeds; it was all I could do to hang on! Even though it looked like madness, he said, "Pedal!"

I worried and was anxious and asked, "Where are you taking me?" He laughed and didn't answer and I started to learn to trust. I forgot my boring life and entered into the adventure and when I'd say, "I'm scared!" he'd lean back and touch my hand. He took me to people with gifts that I needed, gifts of healing, acceptance, and joy. They gave me gifts to take on my journey, my Lord's journey and mine.

And we were off again. He said, "Give the gifts away; they're extra baggage, too much weight." So I did to the people we met, and I found that in giving I received, and still our burden was light.

I did not trust him at first, in control of my life, I thought he'd wreck it; but he knows bike secrets, knows how to make it bend to make sharp corners, knows how to jump to clear high rocks, and knows how to fly to shorten scary passages.

And I am learning to be quiet and peaceful in the strangest places, and beginning to enjoy the view, and the cool breeze on my face, with my delightful constant companion, Jesus Christ.

And when I'm sure I just can't do anymore, he just smiles and says…"Pedal."

(Author Unknown)

This is a great description of "The Journey of Faith." I invite you to join me for the next forty days as we focus on faith. This book is a study of Hebrews 11, and each chapter discusses a different aspect of faith. My goal is to help you develop and strengthen your faith. Perhaps you are standing at a fork in the road, just as I was in Jamaica. Will you walk by fact or will you walk by faith? Are you struggling with God's purpose for your life? Is there a part of you that wants to leave the comfort zone of the ordinary to pursue the extraordinary plans of God? I pray that God might use His Word to stir within you as He did me over twenty years ago. Come and join me as we begin "The Journey of Faith."

1

WHAT IS FAITH?

Now faith is being sure of what we hope for and certain of what we do not see.
(Hebrews 11:1)

Do you remember your first roller coaster ride? I'll never forget the first time I went to Disney World and climbed aboard Space Mountain. I was told it was the scariest roller coaster ever, and the most fun. I was scared to death as I waited in line. What sets this roller coaster apart from others is that you ride Space Mountain in the dark. You cannot see where you are going. You are not prepared when it suddenly goes down, makes a quick turn to the right, or does an upside-down loop. You feel as if you are entering the unknown, which is part of the adventure.

As I debated whether or not to ride Space Mountain, I concluded the adventure of the ride was worth the risk. Deep down, I was sure the ride was safe. Even though I couldn't see where I was going, I was certain I would arrive safely at my destination. So I climbed aboard. When the ride began, it was all I could do to hold on. I found myself gasping for breath as I careened through the darkness. It was indeed the scariest ride of my life. Before I knew it, the ride ended. I crawled out of the car, walked outside, looked into the eyes of my friends and said, "What a ride! What an awesome ride!"

Riding Space Mountain helped me understand faith. Faith is being sure of your safety, even when you are scared. Faith is being certain you will arrive at your destination even if you cannot see where you are going. Faith is a roller coaster ride of ups and downs, twists and turns, with complete assurance that you will arrive at your ultimate destination. And once your ride is over, you will look at your friends and say, "What an awesome ride!"

Definition Of Faith

The Bible defines faith as being sure of what you hope for and certain of what you do not see (see Hebrews 11:1). I like the way Jim Cymbala explains this verse in his book *Fresh Faith*. He teaches that there are two important points regarding faith in this definition. First, faith deals with *future things* ("what we hope for"). Second, faith deals with *invisible things* ("what we do not see").[1] So, faith deals with future things, which are promised by God. These promises will be realized, even if there is no visible evidence at this time.

Hebrews 11:1 teaches you can be sure of what you hope for. The word "hope" is used carelessly today. I have been known to say, "I hope I make a hole in one when I play golf this weekend," or "I hope the New Orleans Saints make it to the Super Bowl this year." It would be a dream come true for me to make a hole in one or for the Saints to play in the Super Bowl. However, these are merely wishes, not true hope. True, biblical hope is "to desire something with *confident expectation of its fulfillment*" (emphasis added).[2]

Hebrews 11:1 also says you can be certain of what you do not see. The world may say, "seeing is believing," but people of faith say, "believing is seeing." It is very natural to trust your five physical senses (what you see, hear, taste, touch, and

13

smell). That is the way the physical (natural) world is designed to work. However, Hebrews 11:1 teaches that faith deals with what is unseen.

What You Do Not See—The Spiritual Realm

Faith works in the spiritual realm beyond your five senses. If you live by your five physical senses, you do not live by faith. Paul encouraged believers that, "We live by faith, not by sight" (2 Corinthians 5:7). In other words, if you can see it, it is not faith. You will never experience the supernatural work of God if you live by what you see happening in the physical world. There is so much more out there than the physical world and its enticements. If you live strictly by sight, you will live a small life. As I stood in line for Space Mountain, I could not see the excitement that awaited me. If I lived by sight, I would never have climbed onto the ride. However, when I believed in something I could not see and acted on that belief, I was able to experience the ride of my life.

Faith starts where your physical senses end. You need to develop your spiritual sense. Eyes of faith are more effective than physical eyes, because eyes of faith enable you to see what is invisible. "So we fix our eyes not on what is seen, but on what is unseen. For what is seen is temporary, but what is unseen is eternal" (2 Corinthians 4:18). Faith believes in the promises of forgiveness, salvation, eternal life in heaven, and an abundant life here on earth. Faith helps me to recognize my life here on earth is an incredible journey and I want to enjoy the ride.

Live By Faith

Faith shows what you believe about God. Most people live

in the physical (natural) world. They put their faith in themselves and wonder why they never see God working. Others want to "claim something by faith" and expect God to give them whatever they want. Faith is not about self-effort. Nor is it a mystical magic trick. Faith connects you to God, and His power, which is provided according to His will (not yours).

To live by faith in God is to live in the spiritual realm. You are saved by faith in God. You are also to live by faith after salvation. When you are certain of what you do not see, you can commit your life to what God says is true. The more you trust God, the greater your faith becomes. The stronger your faith, the more you experience God in your daily life. The more you experience God in your life, the more you know and trust Him. This is an amazing cycle that God wants you to experience again and again. It will lead you toward spiritual maturity.

Tony Evans, in his book *Life Essentials,* says the following:

> A practical definition of faith I like is acting like it's so even when it's not so, in order that it might be so, just because God said so. Now you may be saying, "But that sounds like I'm supposed to pretend something is real when it isn't." Oh no, this is not pretending. We're talking about believing that what God says is true even when no evidence is available. And the way you know you believe it is when you act on it.[3]

That's how I made it through the roller coaster ride at Disney World. I was scared to death, but I kept telling myself God was in control. I trusted everything would be okay, and I knew that when the ride was over I'd be glad I took the risk. Although I truly believed this, my hands were still shaking and my heart was pounding. I behaved like I was calm, even when I wasn't, because I was certain the ride was both safe and enjoyable. In my own way, I acted in faith as I climbed aboard Space Mountain.

So what is faith? Faith is being sure of what you hope for and certain of what you do not see. It is an inner confidence that helps you believe God is in control of all things and you will be okay as long as you trust in Him. As you begin this journey of faith, you must decide whether or not you want to climb aboard the roller coaster. It is totally up to you. You can play it safe and observe from a distance, or you can exercise your faith and climb aboard. If you choose to live by faith, you must know up front that there will be ups and downs, twists and turns. You will experience excitement, sorrow, joy and pain along the way. But when you arrive at your final destination, you will be able to say, "What a ride! What an awesome ride!"

Strengthen Your Faith

Reflect on your life and describe how the journey of faith is like a roller coaster ride.

Do you currently live by faith or by sight? Name one thing you can do right now, which will require you to live by faith.

Meditate on Hebrews 11:1. This is a terrific verse because it provides the very definition of faith.

2

HOW TO PLEASE GOD

Now faith is being sure of what we hope for and certain of what we do not see. This is what the ancients were commended for.
(Hebrews 11:1-2)

How do you please God? What can you do to gain His approval? Years ago, churches gave annual award pins for perfect attendance in Sunday School. Each year, those who had not missed a Sunday, were awarded pins in front of the entire congregation. One lady accumulated ten pins, which represented ten years of perfect attendance. She never missed a Sunday. She may have had the flu, or double pneumonia, but she was in Sunday School every week spreading the gospel and her germs! This woman planned her entire life around Sunday School. She did not take a vacation over a weekend in ten years.

Although her goal of perfect attendance began as a noble endeavor, it eventually became an obsession. Her entire spiritual life revolved around Sunday School attendance. This woman thought that adding another pin was a sure-fire way to please God. She was living under a "works" doctrine because she thought she could earn God's favor.

There are many people in the church today who are just like this woman. They go to church, join a small group, and maybe even participate in the men's ministry. When people ask about their faith, they respond by telling all the things they "do" for God.

Too many people mistakenly believe you please God by doing, working, and performing in life. You may please people this way, but it is not the way to please God. The Bible very clearly teaches that you please God through faith alone. This is what separates Christianity from religion. Religion is often defined as man's attempt to reach or please God. Christianity is responding to God when He reaches down. You please God when you respond by faith to what He has done. Today's Scripture reinforces that even the ancients were commended, or approved by God, through faith.

The Desire To Be Approved

The Message Bible uses the word "distinguished" in Hebrews 11:2: "The act of faith is what distinguished our ancestors, set them above the crowd." One of the definitions for distinguish in Webster's dictionary is, "to make famous or eminent." The word strikes a cord because the desire to be distinguished starts at a very early age. Everyone desires to become famous at some point in life. Children want to be distinguished for their athletic ability, or for their musical talent. In fact, if you ask a group of ten year olds what they want to do when they grow up, most will say they want to be a famous actor/actress, or a professional athlete. My son has high aspirations in life. I remember asking him what he wanted to be when he grew up. He said, "Dad, I want to be a doctor, an astronaut, or work at the doughnut shop!"

Adults are no different. Some individuals are distinguished because of their earning potential, others for their physical appearance. Many awards include the term distinguished. Most universities honor a Distinguished Alumni of the Year. Public schools choose a Distinguished Educator. The military awards the Distinguished Service Medal. The list is endless. The bottom line is, people desire to be distinguished—to be set above the crowd. It is human nature to seek approval.

Whose Approval Do You Seek?

The question of the day is: "Whose approval do you seek?" Do you seek the approval of men or of God? Jesus said in John 5:41, "I do not accept praise from men." Many of your struggles on the journey of faith result from attempting to please people instead of God. Do you ever find yourself grading your Christian life based on the role you play in the church and the hours of service you give to Christian organizations? If you are not careful, you will become a people-pleaser instead of a God-pleaser. Someone once said, "If you please God, it doesn't matter who you displease. If you displease God, it doesn't matter who you please." As you embark on the journey of faith, strive for the praise of God, not the praise of men.

When men praise you, you begin to develop pride. Pride is defined as "an excessively high opinion of oneself; conceit."[1] The Bible teaches that God hates pride (see Proverbs 8:13). Pride causes you to think more highly of yourself than you ought. This was true even in the Old Testament. The Pharisees were held in high esteem in their culture. However, these very "religious" people were unable to see the Son of God standing before them. Jesus told them, "How can you believe if you accept praise from one another, yet make no effort to obtain the praise that comes from the only God?" (John 5:44).

Saved By Grace Through Faith

Grace is the basis for salvation, and it provides the motivation to live a life totally committed to God. This is true now, and was true for the ancients in the days of old. What is grace? Grace is traditionally defined as the "unmerited favor of God."

What does that mean? It means God does for you what you cannot do for yourself. It is receiving what you do not deserve, what you cannot earn.

"For it is by grace you have been saved, through faith—and this not from yourselves, it is the gift of God—not by works, so that no one can boast" (Ephesians 2:8-9). Grace has always been the foundation of a relationship with God. Old Testament believers were saved by the grace of God. New Testament believers are also saved by grace. New Testament grace is obtained through faith in Jesus Christ. Salvation is not by your works. You cannot follow a long list of rules, like the Pharisees, and be deemed worthy by God. You cannot earn the right to go to heaven. It is a gift. You have the choice whether to accept or decline the gracious offer. But the only way to be approved by God is to accept the grace gift God offers—faith.

I often talk with people about making a commitment to Christ and they say things like, "I can't come to Christ now. I have too many problems in my life. Let me get these problems straightened out and then I'll come to Christ." Or they say, "Pastor, I can't come to God now because my life is a mess. Let me get my life together and then I'll make that decision." Statements like these make me very sad, because I know they will never give their life to Christ.

The journey of faith starts where you are right now. God doesn't tell you to get a haircut or change your clothes before you come to Him. He doesn't expect you to be transformed before you give Him your life. He just asks you to accept His free gift. If you wait until you get your life together, it will never happen. Even if you were able to straighten your life out, pride would cause you to see no need for Him.

The beautiful thing about grace is that God accepts you just as you are. He does for you what you could never do for yourself. The Bible never tells you to get your act together before you are saved. Scripture teaches that you come to God just as you are and allow Him to change you according to His plans in His timetable. That is God's grace.

Approved By Faith

So how do you please God? There is nothing you can do to earn His approval. Religious activity cannot save you. Following a list of rules and regulations is not what God desires. God is pleased when you respond by faith to what He has done. Jesus Christ died on the cross to pay the price for your sins. You please God when you trust in Him, not your own deeds.

You receive the approval of God by faith, and faith is only available to you because of grace. This was true for the ancients and is true for you today. There has never been any other way. Faith is the only way. When you put your faith in God, and trust Him completely, you are approved. May you remember every day that faith, and faith alone, is the reason that you are commended.

Strengthen Your Faith

What traits does the world look for when commending or distinguishing people?

How do you receive God's approval?

What is the difference between a God-pleaser and a people-pleaser?

Take time today to meditate on the following statement: "If you please God, it doesn't matter who you displease. If you displease God, it doesn't matter who you please."

3

THE POWER OF GOD

By faith we understand that the universe was formed at God's command, so that what is seen was not made out of what was visible.
(Hebrews 11:3)

Power. Everyone wants power of some sort. There is economic power, social power, the power of a good education, and nuclear power. Never forget political power. The United States is a super power. Others want to destroy the United States because it has power. There is also the power of nature.

I grew up on the coastline of the Gulf of Mexico. Many family members and close friends lost their homes, cars, and all of their earthly possessions in Hurricane Katrina. The town where I grew up was reduced to a pile of rubble. I visited the Mississippi Gulf Coast after the hurricane and was shocked by the magnitude of the devastation. It was like nothing I had ever seen before. So much power, but none of it compares to the power of God.

God Is All-Powerful

God is omnipotent. Omnipotence means God is all-powerful. Put more simply, there is nothing God cannot do. God can create a universe with His spoken word. He can calm the winds and divide the seas. He is able to feed over 5,000 people with two small fish and five loaves of bread.

The world does not want to admit there is a Creator with the power to do anything. To do so would remove mankind from the center of the universe. However, the Bible teaches very clearly that God can do anything. His power is unlimited.

God Spoke

Hebrews 11:3 says that the universe was formed at God's command. "Commanded" in Hebrews 11:3 is translated from the Greek word "rhema" which means word. Each day of creation in Genesis chapter 1 starts with the words, *"And God said."* And. God. Said. Three simple words tell how the universe was created. God spoke, or commanded, the universe into existence. This is the order in which He created the world:

Day 1—Light and Darkness
Day 2—Sky
Day 3—Plants, Land, and Sea
Day 4—Sun, Moon, and Stars
Day 5—Fish and Birds
Day 6—Animals and People

Psalm 33:9 says, "For he spoke, and it came to be; he commanded, and it stood firm." When God spoke, it happened. When he commanded, the results were instantaneous. He did not need complicated blueprints to create the world. He did not work with leading experts in the field of construction. He did not even break a sweat. He simply spoke. It was effortless for God. Everything is effortless for Him, because the Creator can never grow tired or weary (see Isaiah 40:28).

Something Out Of Nothing

Hebrews 11:3 also teaches that what you see was made out

of something invisible. That means God created something out of nothing. It takes amazing power to speak something out of nothing. Genesis 1:2 uses the words formless, empty, and dark to describe the pre-creation state. Nothing existed prior to creation.

We live in the city of Las Vegas, which is presently in an incredible housing boom. Construction continues at break-neck speed. All of this new construction requires raw materials: lumber, concrete, pipes, wiring, etc. Try to put your mind around the fact that God needed absolutely nothing to create this very complex world, and universe.

The fact that God made something out of nothing is a very important point. If *anything* existed prior to creation, it would also be self-existent. To be self-existent is to be equal with God.

The Bible teaches that God is the great I AM (see Exodus 3:14). Yahweh, the personal name for God, is derived from the Hebrew word for "I AM." This shows God alone is in the eternal present tense. God has no starting point. God has no end. Psalm 90:2 says, "Before the mountains were born or you brought forth the earth and the world, from everlasting to everlasting you are God." God alone is self-existent. Therefore, only God can create something out of nothing.

Do Not Be Deceived About Creation

Psalm 89:11 says, "The heavens are yours, and yours also the earth; you founded the world and all that is in it." The Bible is *very clear* about the origin of creation. It is God's creation. He spoke it in to being with His own, eternal power.

Many people do not understand creation. Science does not want to admit the existence of God. Science proposes a myriad of explanations (e.g. the Big Bang, evolution, etc.) in an effort to leave God out of creation.

Do not allow them to confuse you with their endless debate.

Colossians 2:8 says, "See to it that no one takes you captive through hollow and deceptive philosophy, which depends on human tradition and the basic principles of this world rather than on Christ." Satan is actively working to lead you away from God with this issue. He creates controversy and loves it when you turn from God to follow the so-called "evidence" of science. Scientific theories on the origin of the universe have changed over time, but the Word of God remains the same. The Bible accurately explains how the world began.

Creation is a faith issue. The greatest truths are discovered by faith. The Bible is Truth, and the Bible is clear on this issue: God is the Creator. You must believe that God created the world by faith. Believe, even if you do not understand creation. Believe, because of your faith. Faith is being sure of what you hope for and certain of what you do not see. Believe, even if you cannot prove it. Believe because you *know* it is true. You know it is true because God says it is so.

Faith In An All-Powerful God

Jeremiah 32:17 says it well: "Ah, Sovereign LORD, you have made the heavens and the earth by your great power and outstretched arm. Nothing is too hard for you." God is all-powerful. Nothing is too hard for Him.

Because God is all-powerful, He can handle any situation in which you find yourself. God is able to do much more than you could ask or imagine, because of His power (see Ephesians 3:20). All things are possible with God (see Mark 10:27). Take comfort in the knowledge that God can do anything—nothing is impossible! Your faith gives you access to God's power. If you want to see God's power at work in your life, you need to be completely committed to Him.

There are really only two options as to how the world began. You can either believe that everything happened by chance and then evolved, or you can believe that the world began as part of a divine plan, the deliberate strategy of Someone much greater than yourself. It is the age-old debate between science and Scripture. Do you believe in evolution or creation? Do you adhere to the Big Bang theory or the Big God theory? It all boils down to whether you believe in the power of man or the power of God.

When Stuart K. Hine wrote the beloved hymn, "How Great Thou Art," he clearly communicated his belief in an omnipotent and powerful God. As for me, I believe God created the world. I see His handiwork whenever I look at a beautiful desert sunset or gaze up at the stars on a clear evening. Even when I find myself in the midst of a thunderstorm or hurricane force winds, I am reminded that nothing compares to the power of God.

Strengthen Your Faith

Explain in your own words how you think the world began.

Someone once told me the first four words in the Bible are the most important. The Bible opens with, "In the beginning God" (see Genesis 1:1). What do these four words say about the power of God in creation?

Because God is all-powerful, He can handle any situation you are facing today. In what area of your life do you need to experience the power of God?

Meditate on the greatness of God. Sing "How Great Thou Art" as a testimony of your faith in God's power.

4

WHAT IT MEANS TO WORSHIP

By faith Abel offered God a better sacrifice than Cain did. By faith he was commended as a righteous man, when God spoke well of his offerings. And by faith he still speaks, even though he is dead.
(Hebrews 11:4)

Several years ago, I attended a Promise Keepers' rally in Las Vegas with thirty men from my church. There were over 10,000 men at the conference, all with the same goal—to worship God. This diverse group stood side-by-side, with hands raised, singing praises to God. It was a powerful expression of worship.

I also remember a time when my mom and I served lunch at a rescue mission on Christmas Day. The shelter was filled with lonely and desperate people who had not slept, bathed or been comfortable for a very long time. There were not 10,000 people working at the mission that day, nor was there any music. But as we served the food and shared our Christmas with them, I believe it was truly a time of worship.

What comes to mind when you hear the word worship? If you are like most people, you think of the obvious choices: singing, prayer, Christian concerts and communion. Although correct, these answers barely scratch the surface. Worship is so much more.

A simple definition of worship is "loving God." Worship is "loving God," by any means you choose. It is giving your very best to Him. In today's Scripture, Cain and Abel each gave a sacrifice to God. I hope you will see that only Abel truly worshiped God. Abel was commended because he gave his very best.

The Sacrifices Of Cain And Abel

Cain and Abel were the children of Adam and Eve. Cain was older than Abel. Cain was a farmer, and Abel a shepherd. Genesis records that "in the course of time" each brother brought an offering (see Genesis 4:3-4). In other words, Cain and Abel worshiped God. Cain and Abel both believed *in God*. They would not, otherwise, have brought an offering to Him.

Cain brought *some* of the fruits of the soil. Abel brought *fat portions* from some of the *firstborn* of his flock. The Lord looked with favor on Abel's offering, but not Cain's (see Genesis 4:3-5).

The Difference Between The Sacrifices

Cain and Abel both believed in God. They both worshiped Him. They both offered a sacrifice. God reacted differently to the worship of the two brothers. The problem was not so much with the sacrifice as it was the heart of their worship. Hebrews 11:4 in the Message Bible says, "It was what he *believed*, not what he *brought*, that made the difference."

Abel offered His sacrifice by faith, which is all that God accepts. Abel loved God with all of his heart. He believed God was worthy of his worship. He honored God by giving his very best. Abel gave God the fat portions from the firstborn of his flock. He gave willingly to the Lord, and he did it with a joyful heart. Because of his faith, God commended Abel as righteous. Cain gave the Lord some of his fruits. He did not give the first and best of what he had. Cain did not love God with all of his heart. He did not honor God with his best possible offering. Cain was more concerned with what he "gave up" than his worship. He gave begrudgingly to God because he felt he had to. Cain offered the facade of worship. God did not look on Cain with favor, because he did not do what was right (see Genesis 4:5-7).

Abel gave what God wanted. His heart was fully devoted to God. Cain gave what he wanted to give. Cain's heart did not belong to God. The difference between Cain and Abel was the state of their heart. God desires your entire heart.

The Role Of Your Heart In Worship

2 Chronicles 16:9a says, "For the eyes of the LORD range throughout the earth to strengthen those whose *hearts are fully committed to him*" (emphasis added). This is such an exciting verse. God is looking for people who are fully committed to Him! He is actively searching, because commitment is important to Him. *God determines commitment by judging the heart.* God longs for worshipers who will give Him their entire heart. Abel gave God his entire heart. His worship was authentic.

Cain appeared to be religious, but he simply went through the motions. His heart was not in it. Cain gave lip service to God. He wanted to come to God, but on his own terms. Matthew 15:8-9a says, "These people honor me with their lips, but their hearts are far from me. They worship me in vain." Cain's worship was not authentic, and was therefore in vain.

1 Samuel 16:7b says, "The LORD does not look at the things man looks at. Man looks at the outward appearance, but the LORD looks at the heart." The bottom line is this: *It is not the*

outward appearance of your worship that matters. God is concerned with your heart.

A great illustration of this is found in Mark 12:41-44. Jesus observed as a crowd placed their offerings into the temple treasury. Many wealthy individuals came by and tossed large contributions into the collection plate. And then a poor widow dropped in two small coins. The Message Bible describes her contribution as "a measly two cents" (v. 42). Yet Jesus noticed her "measly" offering. He knew the widow's heart was fully devoted to God. Jesus said to His disciples, "I tell you the truth, this poor widow has put more into the treasury than all the others. They all gave out of their wealth; but she, out of her poverty, put in everything—all she had to live on" (Mark 12:43-44).

Love God And Give Him Your Best

I think that widow understood what it means to worship God. As you continue on your journey of faith, I hope you realize that worship is not a posture or a position. Worship is not how many times you attend a church service. Worship is not a style of music or how you partake of communion. Worship is simply loving God and giving your very best to Him.

Colossians 3:23 is a great verse that is very meaningful to me. It says, "Whatever you do, work at it with all your heart, as working for the Lord, not for men." Friends, if you can comprehend this, it can help you understand what the Bible teaches about worship. Worship is giving your best to God, in whatever you do in life. This means that if you are a secretary, you are a secretary for God. If you are an accountant, you are an accountant for God. If you are a teacher, you are a teacher for God. So give your very best to God. That's what Abel did, and you can as well.

Strengthen Your Faith

Explain in your own words what it means to worship God.

How did Abel's worship differ from Cain's?

How can you worship God today at work? At school? At home?

Read Colossians 3:23. Meditate on this verse today.

5

WALKING WITH GOD

By faith Enoch was taken from this life, so that he did not experience death; he could not be found, because God had taken him away. For before he was taken, he was commended as one who pleased God.
(Hebrews 11:5)

When Lisa and I were dating, one of our favorite activities was to go on long walks together. It was on these walks that we really got to know one another. When we walked, there were no outside distractions, such as movies or people, vying for our attention. It was just the two of us. In the beginning, our conversations were superficial. But over time they became more personal and intimate. Fifteen years later, I still treasure those times we went walking together.

Enoch

Last month I met a man named Enoch. He is the father of a member here at Green Valley Baptist Church. Enoch is an unusual name but it is not an unfamiliar one. When he introduced himself as Enoch, my first response was, "Do you walk with God?" In the Bible, the name Enoch is tied to walking with God. The story of Enoch is briefly mentioned in the book of Genesis.

> When Enoch had lived 65 years, he became the father of Methuselah. And after he became the father of Methuselah, Enoch walked with God 300 years and had other sons and daughters. Altogether, Enoch lived 365 years. Enoch walked with God; then he was no more, because God took him away. (Genesis 5:21-24)

Walk With God

The Bible says that Enoch walked with God for three hundred years. In the Amplified Bible, "walk with God" is defined as habitual fellowship with God. "Enoch *walked [in habitual fellowship]* with God" (Genesis 5:22 AB, emphasis added). A habit is something you do automatically, again and again. Fellowship is the process of getting to know someone, to spend time together. Habitual fellowship with God, then, is an intimate, personal and on-going relationship with God. When you have this type of relationship with God, you know Him well. Because you know Him, you trust and obey Him.

Faith is more than simply giving lip service to God and saying that you are a Christian. To live an authentic Christian life, you must walk with God. To walk with God means to spend time with God and desire to know Him better. When you choose to walk with God, you allow Him into the inner parts of your life. You give Him control and ask Him to guide and direct your steps. You depend on God for everything.

Time Alone With God

Walking with God refers to spending time alone with God. It is not easy to walk with God. It requires tremendous spiritual discipline. But if you desire to grow in your Christian life, it is imperative that you spend time alone with God each day.

Just as you cannot get into physical shape by walking once a week, you cannot get into spiritual shape by simply attending a church service on Sunday. You must make time alone with God a priority...everyday. Even Jesus, the Son of God, knew He needed to spend time alone with God in order to accomplish His will. Numerous times in the Bible you will find that Jesus arose early in the morning, to be alone with God. It was the source of His strength, and how He prepared for His day.

Think about it. Would a violinist play in a concert without tuning her violin? No. And a Christian should never attempt to live a day without first getting in tune with God.

I view time alone with God sort of like a heavenly gas station. Just as a car cannot run without gasoline, neither can a Christian function properly without a daily time alone with God. I once heard a faithful Christian say, "If I miss one day of my quiet time, God knows it. If I miss two days, I know it. If I miss three days of my time alone with God, everybody knows it!"

I don't know about you, but I need my daily time alone with God. As I think about the times in my life when I felt closest to God, they often involved walking: at the beach, along a mountain trail, or down a quiet street. Wherever I was, I viewed the time alone as an opportunity to get to know Him better.

During hard times, when I shared my troubles and concerns with God, my faith reassured me. I knew God was with me and that He would take care of me. This faith did not just happen. It took many long walks along the journey of life to develop.

When you walk with God, you are never alone. There may be times when you feel lonely, but you are never alone. When you live by faith, God promises to walk by your side at all times. And if necessary, he will carry you through the difficult times.

Walking By Faith Pleases God

Enoch pleased God because of his faith. Enoch never physically saw God, but he *knew* God. He *walked* with God. Because Enoch walked with God, he had a close relationship with God. I once heard it said that after a particularly long walk, God turned to Enoch and said, "Enoch we have walked so far today, we are closer to My house than to yours. Why don't you just come home with Me today?" And on that day Enoch was no more, because God took him away.

As you continue on your journey of faith, time alone with God is essential to your spiritual growth. When you walk with God, your relationship with God will grow. And when you go through times of sorrow and trouble, you can know that He will carry you, too.

Strengthen Your Faith

What are some obstacles that prevent you from regularly spending time alone with God?

Schedule a time alone with God each day. Allow nothing to interfere with your heavenly appointment.

Each time you meet with God, record the time, place, and a few things you discussed. Check this journal in a week, and again in a month, to see how you are doing.

Reflect on when God has carried you through difficult times. Thank Him for walking with you.

6

GOD-PLEASING FAITH

And without faith it is impossible to please God, because anyone who comes to him must believe that he exists and that he rewards those who earnestly seek him.
(Hebrews 11:6)

It was a hot and dry summer in the desert of west Texas. There had been no rain for months, and the farmers and ranchers were in desperate need of rain. A local pastor decided to call the town to prayer, specifically asking that God send rain to their community. Sunday morning, he announced that a special prayer service would be held on Tuesday evening at the church. His sermon that morning was on faith, and how everyone should pray expecting God to answer. When Tuesday came, the church was filled with farmers, ranchers, and many other people from the community. Before he began his prayer the preacher asked, "Do you have faith? Do you believe God will answer our prayer for rain?" The crowd answered with a resounding yes. The pastor then replied, "Well if you all believe that God is going to send rain, then why didn't you bring your umbrellas?"

I like the way Eugene Peterson paraphrased this verse: "It's impossible to please God apart from faith. And why? Because anyone who wants to approach God must believe both that he exists and that he cares enough to respond to those who seek him" (Hebrews 11:6 MSG).

The Two-Stage Process To God-Pleasing Faith

In Hebrews 11:2, you learned that faith is the only way to please God. The book of Hebrews was originally written to Jewish Christians. Some were contemplating a return to Judaism. Hebrews 11:6 serves as a warning, to caution those who were questioning their faith in Christ. Verse 6 provides the two-stage process required for God-pleasing faith. First, you must believe that He exists. Second, you must believe God cares enough to respond to those who seek Him (i.e. have a personal relationship with God).

Stage 1—Believe That God Exists

The first stage in your journey to God-pleasing faith is to believe that God exists. This means you believe in the one, true, living God. The God you believe to exist *must* be the Father of Jesus Christ. You have to believe that Jesus was sent to redeem you.

This is a crucial point. Most people in the world acknowledge that there is a God. However, few are willing to accept Jesus as their Savior. The argument goes, "All roads lead to heaven, just find the approach that works best for *you*." This idea sounds so good: all of the different religions and philosophies of the world provide a way to God. It is very open-minded, and very inclusive. In reality, this argument is part of Satan's plan to keep you from the kingdom of God. It causes you to miss God's required path to salvation—faith in Jesus Christ.

Man wants to take the popular, easy route. Jesus said, in Matthew 7:13, "Enter through the narrow gate. For wide is the gate and broad is the road that leads to destruction, and many enter through it. But small is the gate and narrow the road that leads to life, and only a few find it."

The world ignores the Truth. The only way to God is set forth in the Bible. Acts 4:12 says, "Salvation is found in no one else, for there is no other name under heaven given to men by which we must be saved." That name is Jesus Christ.

The first stage in your journey to God-pleasing faith is to believe that God exists. But this is only a starting point. James 2:19 says, "You believe that there is one God. Good! Even the demons believe that—and shudder." Demons have first-hand knowledge of God. They lived with Him in heaven (as angels) until they joined Satan in his rebellion. They definitely believe God exists, but they do not have God-pleasing faith.

Stage 2—Have A Personal Relationship With God

Once you believe that God exists, you come to the second phase on your journey to God-pleasing faith. Stage two says that you must believe God cares enough to respond to those who seek Him. The ranchers of west Texas believed that God was able to send rain, but they did not really believe that He would. If they did, they would have brought their umbrellas!

The Bible clearly teaches that God responds to those who seek Him. "I love those who love me, and those who seek me find me" (Proverbs 8:17). Jeremiah 29:13 says, "You will seek me and find me when you seek me with all your heart." The Hebrew word "baqash" is translated "seek" in both Old Testament verses. Baqash means, "to seek to find something." The Greek word "ekzeteo" is translated "seek" in Hebrews 11:6. Ekzeteo means, "to seek out or after, to search for."[1]

The first way God responds to you when you seek Him is with forgiveness of sin and the promise of eternal life. This happens when you ask Jesus into your heart. This pleases God. But salvation is only the beginning of God-pleasing faith.

To continue to please God, you must have fellowship with Him. You just finished studying Enoch, who is known as one who pleased God (see Hebrews 11:5). Enoch pleased God because he walked with Him in habitual fellowship. Enoch knew God. God wants to have a personal relationship with you. God wants to be your reason for living. When you have a personal relationship with God, you know Him, trust Him, and obey Him. The more you get to know Him, the more He will reveal Himself to you. As you learned during your study of Hebrews 11:1, this is an amazing cycle that God wants you to experience again and again. It will lead you toward spiritual maturity. Spiritual maturity is very pleasing to God.

God's Rewards

In Hebrews 11:6, it says that God rewards those who seek Him (NIV). This is a promise. Rewards? What does that mean? There are two types of rewards: free and earned. The first reward God gives is salvation (forgiveness of sin and eternal life). This reward is free to all who accept His gift. It is by grace and cannot be earned (see lesson on Hebrews 11:2). The second reward is your inheritance in the kingdom of God. This second reward is not free. It is determined by your faithfulness to God during your mortal lifetime.

Hebrews 4:1 says, "Therefore, since the promise of entering his rest still stands, let us be careful that none of you be found to have fallen short of it." God's rest is the inheritance you will receive in heaven, which is determined by your faithfulness to God during your mortal lifetime. It is possible to be a Christian and not receive the full inheritance that was available to you.

Allow me to illustrate: When my grandfather died, I remember the discussion about how his inheritance was divided. There were five children or stepchildren who were legal heirs, but one child received the bulk of the estate. As an outside observer, I knew that this son was the primary caregiver in the final years of my grandfather's life. The others were heirs, but because of the deeds he performed for his father, he received a greater portion of the inheritance.

So it is with God. As His adopted child, you are an heir to the kingdom, and will receive eternal life in heaven. But the actual reward you receive in heaven is dependent upon the deeds you perform here on earth.

God will use the Bible, which is Truth, to judge your works (see Hebrews 4:12-13). Some will receive their full inheritance at the judgment. Others will see their works incinerated because of false motives, a race that was not completed, etc. To receive your full inheritance you must be seriously committed to the cause of Christ. You must be faithful. It does not require you to be in a high-profile position, or some type of super-Christian. In fact, the opposite will often be true. Jesus said in Matthew 19:30, "But many who are first will be last, and many who are last will be first." God sees the little things that may seem to go unnoticed in this world. You will be repaid at the resurrection of the righteous (see Luke 14:14).

God-Pleasing Faith

Without faith it is impossible to please God. Faith is the requirement to please God. Faith is needed to enter heaven, and faithfulness is required to receive your inheritance. Live your life by faith, and live it faithfully to the very end.

Strengthen Your Faith

According to Hebrews 11:6, what is impossible?

Why must the God you believe in be the father of Jesus?

Why is salvation only the beginning of God-pleasing faith?

7

FAITH THAT OBEYS GOD

By faith Noah, when warned about things not yet seen, in holy fear built an ark to save his family. By his faith he condemned the world and became heir of the righteousness that comes by faith.
(Hebrews 11:7)

About ten years ago, I was speaking on faith and obedience and used a volunteer to illustrate my point. I had a chair on the platform, and asked a college student named Jeff to stand on the chair and cross his arms. Standing behind him were two strong men. The purpose of the exercise was for Jeff to demonstrate his faith. The two men said, "Fall backward, and you will be caught." With almost no hesitation, Jeff fell backward into the arms of the two strong men, thus demonstrating his faith in the men.

We then placed a blindfold on Jeff and asked him to climb back on the chair. He stood erect, crossed his arms, and prepared to fall. This time, two different men stood behind Jeff. The first two moved in front of him and said, "Fall backward, and you will be caught." Because Jeff couldn't see, and because the voices he heard were in front of him, he did not fall back as commanded. Again, the two men in front of him said, "Fall backward and you will be caught." Jeff paused and asked them if they were sure he would be all right. The men said, "We are sure. Fall backward and you will be caught." With that, Jeff stiffened his body and fell backward into the arms of the two men behind him.

Jeff demonstrated his faith when he obeyed the command to fall while blindfolded. This story reminds me of Noah. When God warned him of things he could not see, Noah trusted God and acted in faith. And when Noah obeyed God, even though he couldn't see the reason for what he was doing, he became righteous in God's eyes.

Noah's Faith

Hebrews 11:7 teaches that Noah was "warned about things not yet seen" (NIV). Other translations say Noah was warned of:

"Something that had never happened before" (NLT),
"Something he couldn't see" (MSG),
"Events of which as yet there was no visible sign" (AB).

All of these translations use different words to state one very important fact: Noah was warned of invisible things. Examine this in light of the definition of faith you learned in Hebrews 11:1. Hebrews 11:1 teaches faith is being sure of what you hope for and certain of what you do not see. You learned in the first lesson that faith deals with future things (what you hope for), and also with invisible things (what you do not see). Faith believes what God says, or in this case "warns," even if there is no visible evidence.

Noah is an amazing example of faith. Noah believed God when He said He would send a flood to destroy the earth. This was astounding when you consider the fact that Noah had no concept of rain. It had never rained before. But when God told Noah He would send a flood, there was no doubt in Noah's mind that it would happen.

Genesis 6:9 says, "This is the account of Noah. Noah was a righteous man, blameless among the people of his time, and he walked with God." Noah was the first person in the Bible to be called righteous. You learned in Hebrews 11:2 that you are approved by God by faith, which is only available because of the grace of a loving God. In Romans 4:5, the Bible says, "faith is credited as righteousness."

Even though God considered Noah righteous, he was still a sinner (see Genesis 9:21). Noah lived in a fallen world and struggled with the same weaknesses and temptations you do today. He was righteous in the eyes of God because of his faith. Like Abel, he loved God with all of his heart. Like Enoch, he walked with God. Because of this, Noah found favor in God's eyes (see Genesis 6:8). Because Noah was faithful with the little things, God entrusted him with something very big.

God's Plan For Noah

God's plan for Noah had two parts. First, Noah was to preach to the wicked. 2 Peter 2:5 calls Noah a "preacher of righteousness." Noah lived during very evil and rebellious times. Genesis 6:5 says, "The LORD saw how great man's wickedness on the earth had become, and that every inclination of the thoughts of his heart was only evil all the time." This grieved the Lord and caused Him pain (see Genesis 6:6). Although the evil pained God, He was patient while the ark was being built (see 1 Peter 3:20).

God gave mankind 120 years to repent from its evil ways (see Genesis 6:3). Because Noah faithfully preached God's message, everyone had the opportunity to know God prior to the destruction. He said it over and over again. "It is going to rain!" The sad reality is that they chose to ignore the message. Only eight people responded to the escape God provided. The rest were destroyed in the flood of God's judgment.

The second part of God's plan was for Noah to build an ark. God gave Noah meticulous instructions on how to build the ark (see Genesis 6:14-16). The ark was 450 feet long, 75 feet wide, and 45 feet high. The length was equivalent to 1 1/2 football fields. The ark was six times longer than it was wide. The height was comparable to a modern four-story building. The ark had three decks. It is estimated the ark could hold 44,000 animals. Noah and his family spent 371 days in the ark.

God also made a covenant (promise) with Noah. "But I will establish my covenant with you, and you will enter the ark—you and your sons and your wife and your sons' wives with you" (Genesis 6:18). God promised Noah he would not be destroyed by the flood.

Noah's Obedient Response To God

How did Noah respond to God's "crazy" plan? "Noah did everything just as God commanded him" (Genesis 6:22). Noah *obeyed* God. In holy fear, he followed God's plan and built an ark. Put another way, Noah *acted* on what he believed. Noah's faith was visible to all because of what he did. For 120 years, he preached and built the ark according to God's specifications. Noah was obedient to his part in God's plan. He allowed God to take care of the rest.

Noah's faith was simply astounding. He built an ark (large ship) nowhere near a major body of water. This appeared ridiculous to everyone outside of his own family. I have often wondered why the people who found Noah's message so absurd, did not reconsider when they saw the animals miraculously come to Noah to board the ark (see Genesis 6:20). Noah obeyed no matter what others said. He did not let public opinion deter him. Noah was willing to look like a fool in the eyes of the world. He knew God's was the only opinion that mattered. Noah knew that the foolishness of God is wiser than man's wisdom (see 1 Corinthians 1:25).

God Still Desires Obedience

God does not change. He is the same yesterday, today and forever (see Hebrews 13:8). God still desires obedience, even if it appears foolish to the world. Noah feared God, and obeyed, as should everyone today. True faith is faith that obeys God, even when the world calls you crazy. You should so fear God that it motivates you to obey Him. You learned in the lesson on Hebrews 11:2 that it is better to please God than to please people. Noah was a God-pleaser, not a people-pleaser. What kind of a pleaser are you?

Obedience is more than a desire to be in God's will. Obedience is an action. Obedience is defined as "a positive, active response to what a person hears."[1] Jeff was obedient when he responded positively to the command that he fall backward, even though he was blindfolded. You demonstrate true faith when you obey God, even when it doesn't make sense. The Bible teaches that obedience comes from faith (see Romans 1:5), and leads to righteousness (see Romans 6:16).

It is when you are obedient to God that you will see Him work. Just as God told Noah to do something "uncomfortable," He also wants you to leave your comfort zone. He wants to use you for noble purposes (see 2 Timothy 2:21). That is the reason you are here on earth right now. God loves to use ordinary people like Noah, or you, because it allows the world to see His power and glory. In obedience, put your faith to work for God.

Strengthen Your Faith

Recall a time when you did something God wanted you to do, even though others thought it was crazy.

What was Noah's response when God told him to build an ark?

Why do you think the people ignored Noah's message of repentance?

Think of an area in your life where you need to obey God by faith, even if it doesn't make sense.

8

THE STEP OF FAITH

By faith Abraham, when called to go to a place he would later receive as his inheritance, obeyed and went, even though he did not know where he was going.
(Hebrews 11:8)

Before Christopher Columbus sailed west from Spain in 1492, most people thought the world was flat and consisted only of Europe, Africa, and Asia. So when Columbus petitioned the king of Portugal for support of his plan to sail west to China, he was denied. Columbus then moved to Spain and submitted the same request to King Ferdinand. He was again denied because his idea seemed so unbelievable. But in 1492, his plan was finally approved and Christopher Columbus sailed off on the adventure of a lifetime. He took a giant step of faith.

I cannot begin to imagine the faith that was required of Columbus and his crew as they sailed west into the unknown. I am sure many of his men thought they would fall off the end of the earth and never be heard of again. But this courageous crew remained faithful to their captain, even when they did not know where they were going. The result was the discovery of a whole new world. North America and South America were discovered because one man chose to step out in faith and follow his dream. Although we now know the Americas were already inhabited, Columbus is the one who opened this new world to Europe and world travel.

Abraham Left Based On God's Promises

In Hebrews 11:8, you are introduced to a man named Abraham, who also stepped out in faith and discovered a new world. Abraham is considered the father of the Jewish nation. The book of Hebrews was written to a Jewish audience. The writer of Hebrews included Abraham to show that the father of their people lived his life by faith. He was given the name Abram at birth, but was later renamed Abraham by God (see Genesis 17:5).

> The LORD had said to Abram, "Leave your country, your people and your father's household and go to the land I will show you.
>
> > "I will make you into a great nation
> > and I will bless you;
> > I will make your name great,
> > and you will be a blessing.
> > I will bless those who bless you,
> > and whoever curses you I will curse;
> > and all peoples on earth
> > will be blessed through you."
>
> So Abram left, as the LORD had told him. (Genesis 12:1-4a)

Abraham was the son of Terah. Terah was a pagan who worshiped other gods (see Joshua 24:2). Despite his family background, God chose Abraham for His plan. God spoke to Abraham. Abraham listened to everything God said.

God promised to make Abraham into a great nation that would bless the entire world. God's promise to Abraham was conditional. It required Abraham to obey, to step out in faith. He had to leave everything behind: everything that was familiar, comfortable, known. What did Abraham do? He did as the Lord told him.

Abraham believed God. Abraham believed if he obeyed God, he would receive greater blessings in the future. So Abraham left. He stepped out in faith. Abraham did not know where he was going, but he left for the land he *knew* God would show him.

Destination Unknown

Hebrews 11:8 says Abraham "did not know where he was going." The Message Bible says he left for "an unknown place," and "had no idea where he was going." The Amplified Bible provides the most interesting translation. It says, "He did not know or trouble his mind about where he was to go." Abraham was not troubled by the fact that he had no idea where he was going, or what he would encounter along the way. In other words, he did not worry about it! It was not Abraham's plan. It was God's plan, and only God knew what the future held. Abraham trusted God and followed Him.

What about you? Do you believe that God has a plan for your life? Do you believe if you obey God and follow Him, that you will receive greater blessings in the future? When you commit to follow God, He promises an adventure of faith. You will experience life to the fullest. But if you fail to obey Him, you will miss out on God's best for your life. The choice is yours. You can follow the way of the world and be deceived by Satan, or you can follow the path that God sets forth. Jesus said it well in John 10:10: "The thief comes only to steal and kill and destroy; I have come that they may have life, and have it to the full." When you trust, obey, and follow God, you will experience life to the full!

From that moment forward, Abraham's life was an adventure of faith. He traveled as a stranger in the land. Whenever God said move, he moved. He lived in complete dependence and obedience to God.

Abraham was originally from Ur in Chaldea. He left Ur for Canaan with his father and family. They settled in Haran (see Genesis 11:31). When Abraham was seventy-five years old, he left Haran for Canaan. He took his wife Sarah, his nephew Lot, and all of their possessions. (His wife's original name was Sarai. She was renamed Sarah by God in Genesis 17:15.) Abraham inquired of God and worshiped throughout his journey (see Genesis 12:7-8).

Take A Step Of Faith

God told Abraham to do one thing: leave. Granted, it was a tough demand. God said, "Give up everything and follow me. And by the way, I will not tell you where you are going." God also promised Abraham a future blessing that was far better than anything Abraham could achieve on his own. Abraham believed God and obeyed. He took a step of faith to follow God, wherever that may lead. The *Life Application Study Bible* footnote for Genesis 12:2 says, "God may be trying to lead you to a place of greater service and usefulness for him. Don't let the comfort and security of your present position make you miss God's plan for you."[1]

God still seeks men and women of obedient faith in the twenty-first century. He is looking for people who are willing to step out in faith...simply because He asked them to. Sometimes that may mean you must leave your safe, familiar surroundings to try something new.

By faith, you must be willing to step out, even if it is into the unknown. This is difficult to do because it is contrary to human nature. Your natural inclination is to want every single detail before you respond to God. Faith does not work that way. Faith requires that you step into unknown territory, knowing that God is always with you (see Matthew 28:20). Faith believes that God's plans are to prosper you and not to harm you (see Jeremiah 29:11).

Why does God require you to take a step of faith? So that you do not become spiritually content. God does not want your faith to hit a spiritual plateau. He wants to strengthen your faith, and this happens as you obey Him. Oftentimes, God will give you just enough information to take one step forward in faith. When you complete the first step, He will provide more detail. After the second step, God will again direct your path. As you keep moving forward, one step at a time, God will continue to guide you. Before you know it, you will find yourself living your life by faith and not by sight (see 2 Corinthians 5:7).

This journey of faith is an adventure. It is the pursuit of a lifetime. It requires you to relinquish control to God and trust Him for the outcome. The good news is that Jesus already knows the way. Trust in Him as you take each step. The end result is always better when you trust Him…and in the process you come to know Him more.

Strengthen Your Faith

How did Abraham exercise faith when he left his country to follow God?

Has an area of your Christian life become too comfortable? Consider that God may be calling you out of your comfort zone.

What might God ask you to leave behind as you embark on a new phase in your journey of faith?

9

FAITH IN GOD'S PROMISES

By faith he made his home in the promised land like a stranger in a foreign country; he lived in tents, as did Isaac and Jacob, who were heirs with him of the same promise.
(Hebrews 11:9)

When I was fifteen years old, I wanted to get a loan to buy a car. I had my eye on a 1966 MGB convertible sports car. The price was $1,500 (a long time ago!). I had $300 in the bank and an old Chevy Malibu worth $200 for a total of $500. I needed to borrow $1,000. My mom made an appointment for me to meet with the vice president of the local bank. She promised that this would be a good experience for me and I would get the loan if I followed her instructions. So I put on my coat and tie, and prepared all the figures to show how I would pay off the loan in twelve months. I listed all of my collateral, which consisted of a bicycle, lawn mower, and the future income from my paper route!

What I didn't know was that my mom had already worked out the deal before I arrived. She co-signed the loan, promising it would be repaid (if not by me, then by her). So as I sweated over getting that loan, I worried for nothing, because it was already a done deal. My mom enabled me to get the loan. She is the one who promised me I would receive the loan and she is the one who promised the bank that the loan would be repaid.

Abraham Believed God's Promise

You learned in the previous lesson that God promised to make Abraham into a great nation that would bless the entire world, *if* Abraham would leave for the land God promised (see Genesis 12:1-3). Abraham believed that God would keep His promise and took a step of faith. Abraham made it to Canaan (the Promised Land) but He never settled the land. God promised the land to his offspring.

God made a covenant (promise) with Abraham that his descendants would receive the land (see Genesis 15:18-21). Abraham lived like a foreigner, like a stranger in the land. He lived a nomadic lifestyle. Abraham, his son Isaac, and his grandson Jacob all lived in tents, which even in those days were not considered permanent dwellings. Abraham never physically possessed the land God promised.

Abraham did, however, possess the land by faith. He believed God's promise that the land would be given to his descendants. So Abraham spent his days as a stranger in the land, waiting patiently on God. He did not complain or question whether God would keep His word. Abraham knew that God would keep His promise.

God's Promises

The Bible is a book of God's promises. In fact, it is jam-packed with His promises. The most important promise in the Old Testament is of the coming Messiah. In the Old Testament, God promised that the Messiah would deliver the people from sin and death, and establish His (spiritual) kingdom.

The word "promise" is used in the Bible over 100 times. These are direct quotes where God says, "I promise…." In addition, there are over 4,110 indirect promises. All of the promises in the Bible fit into one of two categories: unconditional, or conditional.

An unconditional promise occurs when God says He will do something regardless of what you do. In 1 John 4:16b, the Bible teaches that "God is love." This is an unconditional promise, because no matter what you think of God, He will still love you. God is love.

A conditional (a.k.a. if/then) promise requires you to do something. God says, "*If* you do this, *then I promise* to do this in return." You must obey God to receive the conditional promise. 2 Chronicles 7:14 is an example of a conditional promise. It says, "*If* my people, who are called by my name, will humble themselves and pray and seek my face and turn from their wicked ways, *then* will I hear from heaven and will forgive their sin and will heal their land" (emphasis added).

The Mosaic Law

You learned in Hebrews 11:2 that many Old Testament Jews could not accept grace as the foundation of their relationship with God. They lived by their own strict interpretation of the Mosaic law (the biblical law code given to Moses by God). Under Mosaic law, you could either obey and be blessed with life, or disobey and be cursed with death (see Deuteronomy 30:19). The Pharisees believed you could follow a long list of rules and be deemed worthy. However, it was not possible for the sacrificial system to take away sins (see Hebrews 10:4). The Bible teaches you cannot earn the right to go to heaven.

The Pharisees' interpretation of Mosaic law was a perversion of its God-intended purpose. God originally gave the law to Moses because He wanted to show His people they could never (by any works) measure up to God's perfect standard. By showing them how they fell short of the excellence God required, the law pointed toward the *Savior* that God *promised*.

The law was intended to show God's plan to restore man to Himself.

Jesus Fulfills God's Promise To Abraham

When Jesus died on the cross as a sacrifice for our sins, He canceled the Mosaic law. "Having canceled the written code, with its regulations, that was against us and that stood opposed to us; he took it away, nailing it to the cross" (Colossians 2:14). Jesus gave a new law—the law of the Spirit of life (i.e. the Holy Spirit). Romans 8:2 says, "Through Christ Jesus the law of the Spirit of life set me free from the law of sin and death."

When Jesus canceled the law of Moses, He provided an uninterrupted connection back to the Abrahamic covenant, which was based on a promise, not the law. The Abrahamic covenant or promise occurred when God called Abraham and promised to make him into a great nation that would bless the entire world. The nation that came from Abraham was Israel. Through Israel, the entire world was blessed by the birth of the Messiah, Jesus Christ. The genealogy at the beginning of Matthew traces Jesus' ancestry back to Abraham to show that God did indeed keep His promise to Abraham. God kept His promise because He is faithful (see Hebrews 10:23).

Christians Are Abraham's Spiritual Descendants

"If you belong to Christ, then you are Abraham's seed, and heirs according to the promise" (Galatians 3:29). This verse teaches that those who accept Jesus as God's Messiah are Abraham's seed (descendants) and are spiritual heirs to God's promise.

God originally made His name known to the world through the nation of Israel (Abraham's biological descendants). He now uses His church, because Christians are Abraham's spiritual descendants. Peter taught that the church, made up of followers of Jesus Christ, is God's holy *nation*. He says in 1 Peter 2:9, "But you are a chosen people, a royal priesthood, a holy nation, a people belonging to God, that you may declare the praises of him who called you out of darkness into his wonderful light." The church, with Jesus as its head, is now the method God uses to spread hope and salvation to a lost world.

Jesus Is The Answer To God's Promises

Jesus is the answer to all of the Old Testament promises of a Savior. In fact, Jesus Christ is the answer to *all* of God's promises. The answer is YES! I like the way the Amplified Bible says it in 2 Corinthians 1:20:

> For as many as are the promises of God, they all find their Yes [answer] in Him [Christ]. For this reason we also utter the Amen (so be it) to God through Him [in His Person and by His agency] to the glory of God.

The Amplified Bible explains that the word "yes" in this verse means, "answer." Jesus answered, or fulfilled, all of God's promises about the Messiah. Because God kept His promise to send a Messiah, you can *know* He will keep every other promise recorded in the Bible. The Bible is filled with the promises of God to His children. Jesus is proof positive that God is faithful. He will keep His word!

Faith In God's Promises

When I think back to the time I sat before the banker, I am reminded that it was not nearly as hard to get the car loan as I thought. I tried to prove myself worthy, and demonstrate how I could pay the loan back all by myself. I later learned that getting the loan had very little to do with me, and everything to do with my mom. She is the reason that I got the loan and the car. In the same way, the answer to all of God's promises is yes. Not because you are worthy or you deserve it, but because of Jesus. Jesus Christ is the reason that you are an heir to the promises of God. If you have placed your trust in Jesus Christ, you can know that all the promises in the Bible are just for you. And you can trust God to keep His promises.

In Hebrews 11:1, you learned that faith deals with future things, which are promised by God. The very definition of faith, then, is to believe God's promises. Faith and God's promises are one and the same. Abraham believed God's promises. So can you. Live your life by faith in God's promises.

Strengthen Your Faith

What comes to mind when you hear the word "promise?"

What did God promise Abraham? How did it affect the way he lived?

Describe a time in your life when someone broke a promise. How did you feel?

Make a list of some of the promises God has made in His Word.

10

CITIZENS OF HEAVEN

For he was looking forward to the city with foundations, whose architect and builder is God.
(Hebrews 11:10)

Someone recently told me that eight of the ten largest hotels in the world are located in Las Vegas. Every year it seems a newer, bigger, and better one pops up, and an older one is torn down. This year, one of the landmark hotels here in Las Vegas was imploded with dynamite to make room for a brand new mega resort. As big and beautiful as these new hotels are, there will come a day when they will be torn down and reduced to rubble. This is yet another reminder of the temporary state of the world in which we live.

Abraham was from the city of Ur. The University of Pennsylvania and the British Museum excavated Ur a few years ago and discovered that Ur may have had the very first high rise buildings. They found wonderful two-story mansions that were single-family dwellings. It is likely that Abraham lived in one of these beautiful homes. But Abraham left Ur to live in a foreign land. He knew that Ur, just like Las Vegas, would one day pass away. What was he looking for? The Bible answers this question in Hebrews 11:10 when it says, "He was looking forward to the city with foundations, whose architect and builder is God."

I believe when Abraham thought about heaven he said to

himself, "That's where I want to live. I will never be at home here. I don't fit in. I will stay here as long as God wants, but I'm looking forward to the day when I get to my real home in heaven." Heaven is the only place where people of faith will ever be at home.

Heaven Is The Ultimate Fulfillment Of God's Promise

Abraham believed that his descendants would one day inherit the land that God promised him. The promised land of Canaan was an Old Testament type designed to illustrate heaven. A type is "a figure, representation, or symbol of something to come."[1] Israel's promised land was designed to point them toward the ultimate fulfillment of God's promise—heaven. The Israelite experience in Canaan, no matter how wonderful, can never compare to heaven. Abraham's true promised land was heaven. Abraham *knew* he was going to heaven. He was confident of this.

The Message Bible says that Abraham kept his eyes on an "unseen city." Abraham did not look forward to an earthly city. He looked forward to an unseen city. The unseen city is heaven. Heaven cannot be seen with your physical eyes. Heaven currently exists in the spiritual realm, which is invisible. Although Abraham could not see heaven, he knew by faith that it did exist. It also says that the unseen city has "real, eternal foundations." This stands in stark contrast to the tents Abraham lived in while on this physical earth. Heaven is permanent. It will be forever and ever (see Revelation 22:5).

Heaven is a city designed and built by God. Heaven is a place that has been planned for all eternity. Jesus said in Matthew 25:34 that the kingdom of heaven was "prepared for you since the creation of the world." It is a beautiful place (see Revelation 21:2) because it is where God lives (see Revelation

21:3). Heaven is also described as very peaceful. There will be no more tears, death, crying, or pain (see Revelation 21:4). You will have a purpose in heaven. As you learned in Hebrews 11:6, you will receive a reward (position or job in heaven) based on your faithfulness to God while on earth. You will assist God in the administration of His kingdom (see Revelation 5:10) in the coming ages (see Ephesians 2:7). Jesus went to prepare a place *for you* in heaven (see John 14:2). The words "for you" show that heaven is more than just a beautiful place. Heaven is warm and welcoming. It is personal.

Ezekiel said the name of heaven is, "The LORD is there" (Ezekiel 48:35). That is the very best part of heaven. It is where God and Jesus are. To be in heaven is to be in the presence of God.

Jesus—The Way To Heaven

Jesus spoke to the disciples about heaven on the night before he was crucified. Bruce Wilkinson said, "As the only person to come from eternity to earth, then return to eternity, Jesus knows the whole truth—past, present, and future—and can give you a one-of-a-kind perspective."[2]

> Do not let your hearts be troubled. Trust in God; trust also in me. In my Father's house are many rooms; if it were not so, I would have told you. I am going there to prepare a place for you. And if I go and prepare a place for you, I will come back and take you to be with me that you also may be where I am. You know the way to the place where I am going….I am the way and the truth and the life. No one comes to the Father except through me. (John 14:1-4, 6)

Jesus said He was leaving to prepare a place for you in heaven. He promised that He would return sometime in the future. Jesus also taught that the way to heaven is certain. There is no ambiguity—Jesus is the way. No one comes to the Father without faith in Jesus Christ. Those who believe in Jesus will receive eternal life (see John 3:16). Jesus, as God's only Son, lived, died, and rose again, so that you may live. He opened the way for you to enter heaven. Because of Jesus, you can look forward to a better place—an eternal city, a heavenly country. If you are a born-again Christian, heaven will be your home for eternity.

Home Is In Heaven

Abraham set his heart and mind on things above (see Colossians 3:1-2) throughout his lifetime. "Things above" refers to heaven. Abraham made God's priorities his priorities. He focused on things of eternal significance rather than living for the here and now. Philippians 3:20 teaches that your "citizenship is in heaven." Abraham changed his citizenship from earth to heaven.

Abraham was content to live in tents while on the earth because he knew he was not a citizen of this world. His citizenship was in heaven, and he longed for his eternal home. He knew that it wouldn't be long before he pulled up stakes and moved into his eternal home in heaven, a mansion built just for him. And best of all, he would never have to move again!

Most people prefer to keep their citizenship on earth. They fix their eyes on the things of this world, which are only temporary. God wants you to live by faith, and fix your eyes on heaven (the unseen). That which is unseen is eternal and lasts forever (see 2 Corinthians 4:18).

In the Sermon on the Mount, Jesus taught:

> Do not store up for yourselves treasures on earth, where moth and rust destroy, and where thieves break in and steal. But store up for yourselves treasures in heaven, where moth and rust do not destroy, and where thieves do not break in and steal. For where your treasure is, there your heart will be also. (Matthew 6:19-21)

"For where your treasure is, there your heart will be also" is a very important truth. God wants you to treasure Him above everything else. Like Abraham, make God's priorities your priorities. Focus on things of eternal significance rather than living for the here and now. You may be familiar with the picture of the dot and the line.

•⎯⎯⎯⎯⎯⎯⎯⎯⎯⎯⎯⎯⎯⎯⎯⎯→

The dot represents your life on this earth. The line represents eternity and goes on forever. You will spend a very brief period of time on this earth (approximately seventy-five years). You will spend eternity in heaven. Eternity is a much longer period of time than seventy-five years. Do not make the mistake of living for the dot. It is very important that you live for the line, because eternity is where you will spend the majority of your time.

God wants you to live for Him alone—His purposes, His glory. Allow Abraham's life of faith to motivate you to live for heaven. Live for the enduring city that is to come. Live your life for the city that will never fade away. Acknowledge that this world is not your home and change your citizenship from earth to heaven. Heaven is your home!

Strengthen Your Faith

Describe heaven in a single sentence.

According to Ezekiel 48:35, what is the best part of heaven?

Read 2 Corinthians 4:18. Describe how it is possible to fix your eyes on the things of this world.

Meditate on your home in heaven and what it will be like to spend eternity in the presence of God.

11

WHEN YOUR FAITH WAVERS

> *By faith Abraham, even though he was past age—and Sarah herself was barren—was enabled to become a father because he considered him faithful who had made the promise.*
> (Hebrews 11:11)

    Have you ever thought that something was impossible even for God? Lee Trevino, the great golfer, was once on the golf course when a bolt of lightning struck nearby. While the other golfers ran for cover, Trevino picked up a golf club and held it over his head. His playing partner asked why he was holding a metal club with lightning all around. Trevino replied, "Don't worry, even God can't hit a one iron!" He believed some things are impossible even for God.

    When you live by faith, you acknowledge that nothing is impossible for God. One of the best definitions of faith I've heard is that "faith is living without scheming." This definition hit me right between the eyes because, even though I have a strong faith, there are many times in my life when I try to help God along to accomplish what I want in life. Have you ever done that? You believe God will find you a husband or a wife, but you take matters into your own hands and start looking for dates in the wrong places. You believe that God will find you a job, but you start embellishing your resume. If you are like me, you have learned the hard way that when you take matters out of God's hands and start scheming, it usually turns into a big mess.

The Scheming Of Sarah

Consider Sarah. Because Sarah was old and barren, she felt it was impossible for God to keep His promise of a son. Her faith wavered. Sarah decided to take matters into her own hands. She developed a plan as recorded in Genesis 16. Sarah reasoned that since God promised Abraham a son, and she could not have children, surely God wanted Abraham to sleep with another (fertile) woman. Sarah told Abraham to sleep with her maidservant Hagar and Abraham agreed.

When Hagar became pregnant, it caused Sarah much grief. Hagar began to despise her barren mistress. In return, Sarah began to mistreat Hagar. By taking matters into her own hands, Sarah had created a huge mess. Things became so bad that Hagar ran away.

The angel of the Lord spoke to Hagar during this difficult time. The angel of the Lord told Hagar to return to Sarah. He promised her that her descendants would be too numerous to count. Hagar was told to name her son Ishmael, and that he would live in hostility with all his brothers. Hagar obeyed the Lord and returned home. When her son was born, she named him Ishmael.

In Genesis 17, God spoke to Abraham about Sarah. He said, "I will bless her and will surely give you a son by her. I will bless her so that she will be the mother of nations; kings of peoples will come from her" (Genesis 17:16). Abraham laughed at this news, as he was already one hundred years old, and Sarah was ninety. God told Abraham that Sarah would have a son by this time next year and they were to name him Isaac. Ishmael was thirteen at this time.

The Lord appeared again to Abraham in Genesis 18. The Lord said He would return this time next year and Sarah would have a son. Sarah was eavesdropping and laughed as she heard this news. The Lord knew that Sarah was listening and that she had laughed at the notion of having a baby. God replied, "Is anything too hard for the LORD?" (Genesis 18:14).

God was gracious and Sarah had a son, just as He promised. Abraham named the baby Isaac. Eventually, Hagar and Ishmael were sent away because of trouble within the family. At that time, God clarified His promise to Abraham. *It was Isaac's descendants that He would make into a great nation that would bless the entire world* (see Genesis 21:12). God promised to make Ishmael's descendants into a nation as well.

Isaac's descendants became the Jewish people, the nation of Israel. Ishmael's descendants became the Arabs. Just as God said, these two nations live in hostility to this very day. The animosity between the Jews and Arabs began at the birth of Isaac and still continues. Because of their belief in Jesus, the ultimate fulfillment of God's promise, that enmity now includes Christians.

Weakened Faith/Unbelief

By her actions, you can see that Sarah felt it was impossible for God to keep His promise of a son. Sarah felt she needed to intervene on God's behalf. She took matters into her own hands, and developed a plan. It sounded very logical on the surface. Sarah probably thought, "God promised Abraham a son, and I am unable to have children. Abraham needs another woman to have this child. I had better go find a woman for Abraham to sleep with."

In essence, Sarah was scheming. She manipulated people and circumstances to "help" God fulfill His promise. She devised a clever scheme to ensure that Abraham had a son. And it worked. Abraham did have a son—just not the son God promised.

So what went wrong in Sarah's life to set into motion this chain of events? It was not that Sarah never had faith. She was unquestionably a woman of faith. In fact, Sarah is the first woman mentioned in the "Faith Hall of Fame" (Hebrews 11). The problem was that she took her eyes off of God and focused them on her situation. She traded in her eyes of faith for physical eyes, which can only see the here and now. This caused her faith to weaken. The bottom line here is this: Sarah's faith wavered. She failed to look past her circumstances to the One who made the promise.

God responded with a question when Sarah laughed at the thought of being a mother in her old age. He asked, "Is anything too hard for the LORD?" (Genesis 18:14). God did this because Sarah had lost sight of Who God is. She forgot His attributes.

First of all, Sarah forgot that God is omnipotent (all-powerful). That means nothing is too hard for God (see Jeremiah 32:17). Sarah felt that her inability to have children could not be reversed. The truth of the matter is that all things are possible with God (see Mark 10:27), no matter how unlikely they appear with your human eyes. There is no situation He cannot handle.

Second, Sarah failed to realize that God is self-sufficient (see Acts 17:25). Sarah knew that God had a plan, and tried to help Him. However, God did not need any help to accomplish His plan. God designed His plan, and He knew how to best bring it to completion.

Third, Sarah did not rely on the fact that God is omniscient (all-knowing). God has perfect knowledge of all things (see Isaiah 40:13-14). From her human vantage point, Sarah did not see the big picture. The problem was that her outlook was very limited. She did not truly grasp the enormity of God's plan.

Finally, Sarah forgot that God does not lie (see Titus 1:2). She doubted God would keep His promise. But the truth is, God will always keep His promise. Hebrews 10:23 says, "Let us hold unswervingly to the hope we profess, for he who promised is faithful." If God promises, it will happen. Sarah's faith was weakened and she allowed her unbelief to affect her actions. She took matters out of God's hands and into her own. Sarah was not obedient to God. Sarah's manipulation did not alter God's plan in any way. Isaac was born, and God blessed the world through his birth. However, Sarah's actions brought much unhappiness and strife into her life. One consequence of her scheme, animosity between the descendants of Abraham's two sons, continues to this very day.

When Your Faith Wavers

If you are like me, you may find it easy to identify with Sarah. You want to believe God's promises, but question, "How can it be?" You have faith, but it is not as strong as you would like.

It is normal to wrestle with unbelief at times. Do not let your feelings and circumstances dictate what you believe. Learn from Sarah and do not try to fix every problem yourself. You will only make the situation worse. Remember that faith never has to scheme. Faith never needs to manipulate people and circumstances. God never needs your help. For those times when you feel your faith wavering and unbelief is creeping back into your life, pray, "I do believe; help me overcome my unbelief!" (Mark 9:24).

Strive for strong faith, which enables you to see beyond your circumstances as you rely on God. You do not need to understand how God will do something. You just need to believe that He will! Wait for God's plan to be fulfilled in His time. In the meantime, focus your eyes on Who God is. God will keep His promise, and His timing is always perfect! And remember the definition of faith mentioned above. Faith is living without scheming.

Strengthen Your Faith

Do you place your faith in God or in circumstances? What circumstances have caused your faith to waver in the past?

Describe a time when you attempted to "help" God by scheming or manipulating circumstances. What was the result?

Sarah lost sight of Who God is, which caused her faith to waiver. In your own words, explain the four attributes of God studied in today's lesson.

Meditate on the phrase "faith is living without scheming." In what area of your life do you need to stop scheming and start trusting God?

12

THE BLESSINGS OF GOD

And so from this one man, and he as good as dead, came descendants as numerous as the stars in the sky and as countless as the sand on the seashore.
(Hebrews 11:12)

What does it mean to be blessed by God? Are you blessed when your business prospers? Are you blessed when you are free of sickness and disease? Are you blessed when you have a nice house and car? Are you blessed when you have a happy family? What does it really mean to be blessed by God?

The Bible speaks often on the topic of God's blessing. The words "bless," "blessed," and "blessing," are translated from the Hebrew word barak or its derivatives. The Amplified Bible defines blessed as, "happy, fortunate, to be envied."

Blessings are very important. Blessings can be physical (e.g. wealth) or spiritual (e.g. peace). The purpose of blessings is to showcase God; to make His name known and bring Him glory. As you are blessed, it allows others to see what God is doing in your life. Blessings allow people to say, "See what God has done!" (Numbers 23:23b).

Abraham Was Blessed By God

Abraham and Sarah thought they would never have any

children, much less have descendants as numerous as the sand on the seashore. But after many years, Abraham and Sarah had a son named Isaac. Isaac was born when both his parents were well past their childbearing years. Isaac was born when Abraham was one hundred and Sarah was ninety years old. Isaac's biological descendants became the Jewish people, the nation of Israel. All Jews, to this very day, are the physical descendants of Abraham.

You learned in Hebrews 11:9 that Christians are Abraham's spiritual descendants. "If you belong to Christ, then you are Abraham's seed, and heirs according to the promise" (Galatians 3:29). Peter taught that Christians (Abraham's seed) are God's holy *nation*. He said in 1 Peter 2:9, "But you are a chosen people, a royal priesthood, a holy *nation*, a people belonging to God, that you may declare the praises of him who called you out of darkness into his wonderful light" (emphasis added).

God kept His promise to make Abraham into a great nation. Today, there are so many believers, that it is impossible to count them all. It would be like trying to count the grains of sand at the beach or the stars in the sky. Impossible! This is an abundant blessing from God.

I remember as a child going to the opening of the movie, *101 Dalmatians*. The theater had a live Dalmatian in a cage for all to see. Each child had the opportunity to guess how many spots were on the puppy. Whoever guessed the exact number of spots would win the puppy as a prize. I sat in front of that cage most of one Saturday afternoon trying to count the spots on that dog. Whenever I counted to about forty-five or fifty, the puppy would move, and I would have to start all over again. I first guessed about seventy-five spots, but soon learned that there were hundreds and hundreds of spots. I decided it was a useless endeavor. It was impossible to count the number of spots on the Dalmatian: there were too many and he kept moving around.

The number of spots on a Dalmatian is miniscule when compared to the quantity of sand on the seashore. God promised Abraham that his descendants would be as numerous as the sand on the seashore (see Genesis 22:17). My human mind cannot even comprehend a number that large. He was indeed a blessed man.

God's Blessing

You may remember God's original promise to Abraham in Genesis 12:2-3 (emphasis added):

> "I will make you into a great nation
>   and I will *bless* you;
> I will make your name great,
>   and you will be a *blessing*.
> I will *bless* those who *bless* you,
>   and whoever curses you I will curse;
> and all peoples on earth
>   will be *blessed* through you."

The words "bless," "blessed," and "blessing," are used five times in these two verses alone. I believe that God desires to bless you, but your choices determine whether or not you will be blessed. Look closely at what the Bible says in Deuteronomy 30:19: "This day I call heaven and earth as witnesses against you that I have set before you life and death, *blessings and curses*. Now *choose* life, so that you and your children may live" (emphasis added).

So how do you receive God's blessing? You need to give God your entire heart. You learned in Hebrews 11:4 that God wants your fully-committed heart (see 2 Chronicles 16:9a). Abraham gave God his complete devotion, and was blessed for his faith. Jesus taught in the Sermon on the Mount that you should, "Seek first his kingdom and his righteousness, and all these things will be given to you as well" (Matthew 6:33). When you make God the most important thing in your life, He will bless you. But how can you be sure that God is the most important thing in your life and therefore receive His blessing?

Worship

First, examine your worship, because the Bible shows a direct connection between worship and blessing. The Amplified Bible says that a blessed man is one who worships the Lord (see Psalm 112:1 AB). In Zechariah 14:17 it says that you must worship to receive rain. Rain is used in verse 17 to represent blessings. Blessings are dependent upon worship.

So what should your worship look like? In the discussion of Cain and Abel in Hebrews 11:4, you learned that Abel gave his very best to God, but Cain gave his leftovers. Abel gave sacrificially from the first of his fruits, while Cain gave out of his excess. God accepted the worship of Abel, but He did not accept Cain's worship. True worship happens when you give God your very best: the best of your time, the best of your talent, and the best of your tithe. True worship pleases God and allows His blessing to rain down on you.

Obedience

Second, check to see if you obey God's Word. The Bible says you will be prosperous and successful if you obey God's Word (see Joshua 1:8). If you want to be blessed, you must do what is written in the Bible. You cannot choose to obey some parts, and disregard others. Deuteronomy 29:9 says that when you carefully follow the terms of the covenant, you will prosper in all that you do. In other words, when you choose to obey all of God's commands, you will be blessed. Does this mean you have to be perfect? No. It simply means you are committed to living by the Bible's principles.

Walk In The Spirit

Third, verify that you walk in the Spirit (see Galatians 5:25 NKJV). The term "walk in the Spirit" means your conduct is controlled by the Spirit. In other words, the Holy Spirit must be in charge of your life. This is also known as being Spirit-filled. Test each aspect of your life to ensure you have given the Spirit complete control of every thought and action. The Bible promises the blessings of life and peace when you allow your mind to be controlled by the Spirit (see Romans 8:5-6).

Ministry

Finally, ask yourself how committed you are to your local church. In Matthew 6:33, Jesus said to seek first His kingdom. That is Jesus' way of saying that the kingdom of God is priority one. But how does the kingdom of God relate to church? The church is how God chose to establish His kingdom on earth. In fact, the church is the pillar and foundation of truth (see 1 Timothy 3:15), which makes it the most important institution on the planet. God is looking for people who are committed to their local church and are willing to do whatever it takes to ensure their church reaches others. Do you commit yourself to His kingdom through your church? The Bible promises that those who are planted in the House of God will flourish (see Psalm 92:13). God will bless those who plant deep roots in their local church.

Blessed To Be A Blessing

God is very gracious to bless you, and when He does, please remember that God's blessing is not for you to hoard. God blesses you so that you will be a blessing to others (see Genesis 12:2). God wants you to use your blessing to influence the world around you, just as Abraham did. He entrusts His blessing to you, so that you can bless others in return.
The purpose of being blessed by God is not to hoard your blessings, but to give them away. You have opportunities every day to bless others with the blessings God has bestowed upon you. You have been blessed to bless others. When you live your life by faith, you are blessed to be a blessing. As you continue on your journey of faith, make it a point to pass along the blessings you receive.

Strengthen Your Faith

How would you define the word "blessed?"

How do you receive God's blessing?

What does God want you to do with your blessing?

List two ways you have been blessed by God. How can you share these blessings with others?

13

STRANGERS ON EARTH

All these people were still living by faith when they died. They did not receive the things promised; they only saw them and welcomed them from a distance. And they admitted that they were aliens and strangers on earth. People who say such things show that they are looking for a country of their own.
(Hebrews 11:13-14)

 Who is your favorite alien? When I was young, there was a popular television program called, "My Favorite Martian." I also remember when Robin Williams first burst on the scene with the television sitcom, "Mork and Mindy." For those of you who are a bit younger, you may remember "ALF," which was a comedy about an alien who had come to earth. But my favorite alien, bar none, is E.T. He was a loveable creature who came to earth, but longed to return to his permanent home in a faraway land.

 The dictionary defines an alien as someone who is from another country, someone who is different in nature, or a stranger in a foreign land. Abraham met every definition of an alien: He lived in a foreign country, he was totally different in nature from the people around him, and he lived as a stranger in a foreign land. Abraham understood that he was merely a visitor on this earth; that his true home was in heaven. He did not fit in with the rest of the world. Abraham's faith in God enabled him to live as an alien in a foreign land until that time when he arrived at his true home in heaven.

Christians Are Aliens Or Strangers In The World

As a believer in Jesus Christ, heaven is your ultimate destination as well. In the meantime, you must live as a temporary resident of this world. The Bible uses several different words to illustrate your relationship to this present world (e.g. "transients," "exiles," "temporary residents," "aliens," and "strangers"). As an alien or stranger in the world (see 1 Peter 2:11), you should be noticeably different than a non-believer.

God does not want you to blend in with your environment. He wants you to literally "counter the culture." He wants you to live as a radical non-conformist. Today, when you hear the words "radical" or "non-conformist," you tend to visualize hippies or left-wing liberals. That was not true when Jesus walked the earth. He was considered radical in His teachings.

Jesus upset both the Roman and Jewish authorities, and turned the religious community on its ear. Jesus was well aware that this earth was not His home. He was a stranger, an alien in this world. Jesus stood in sharp contrast to the world in the way He thought and the way He lived. Some people thought Jesus was brilliant, and others called Him crazy. One thing is certain: He did not conform to the ways of the world. He stood out in the crowd.

Unfortunately, many Christians do not appear much different than society-at-large. Their values and lifestyle are more influenced by the world than by their faith. Jim Cymbala said, "I fear that too often we are being converted and discipled by the world rather than the other way around."[1] I have also heard this described as "the carnalization of the church."

Jesus taught that if you are a true disciple, you should not feel comfortable living in this world. In fact, if you live your life as a devoted follower of Christ, the world will hate you. In John 15:18-19, Jesus said,

> If the world hates you, keep in mind that it hated me first. If you belonged to the world, it would love you as its own. As it is, you do not belong to the world, but I have chosen you out of the world. That is why the world hates you.

As a Christian, you must choose how you will live. You can live for God, as a stranger on this planet; or you can live for self, and blend in with the rest of the world. It is completely up to you.

Do Not Conform

One of my life verses is found in Romans 12:2. It says, "Do not conform any longer to the pattern of this world, but be transformed by the renewing of your mind. Then you will be able to test and approve what God's will is—his good, pleasing and perfect will."

In the King Rob version, I paraphrase this verse to say, "Dare to be different. Don't be like everybody else. Let God use you, and make you into the best you could ever be." Please remember that you are in the world, but not of the world. Don't blend in. Stand out, in sharp contrast to the people of the world.

A young boy was given a special Easter gift. He received a baby chicken, which had been dyed bright purple. The little boy called it his "Easter" chicken. Because of its purple color, this chicken looked different than all the other chickens on the farm. He definitely stood out in a crowd.

After a few weeks, something interesting began to happen.

The bright purple dye on the Easter chicken began to fade, and he started looking more like the other chickens. Over time, all of the purple dye disappeared. Without the dye, it was impossible to distinguish the Easter chicken from all the other chickens in the yard. He no longer stood out in the crowd.

Many Christians today have become just like the Easter chicken. They profess their faith in Christ, and embark on the journey of faith with tremendous excitement. They are distinguished because of their faith and it shows—they definitely stand out in a crowd. But down the road, their initial enthusiasm begins to fade and they start to blend in with the pack. Eventually, they reach a point where there is no visible difference between them and the world. This is not what God intended.

Dare To Be Different

So what about you? Do you stand out in a crowd or do you blend right in? Are you a stranger in this world, or do you feel at home? As a Christ-follower, you are called to live as a stranger or an alien in this world. Remember, you are only a temporary resident here. Your eternal home is in heaven. Be careful not to conform to the ways of the world during your short stay here on earth. Instead, allow your faith to showcase God. Jesus said you should, "Let your light shine before men, that they may see your good deeds and praise your Father in heaven" (Matthew 5:16).

As you live your life by faith, dare to be different than society-at-large. Remember that you are to counter the culture, and stand in stark contrast with the world. I pray that you will not blend in with the crowd, because when you live as a stranger or alien, you give people an opportunity to see the difference Jesus Christ has made in your life.

Strengthen Your Faith

What does it mean to be an alien or a stranger on the earth?

In John 15:18-19, what does Jesus say about your standing in the world?

The story of the Easter chicken describes many Christians today. In what ways do you blend in with the crowd?

Meditate on Romans 12:2. Ask God to transform your life so you can live as a counter-culture Christian.

14

WHAT MAKES YOU DIFFERENT?

> *All these people were still living by faith when they died. They did not receive the things promised; they only saw them and welcomed them from a distance. And they admitted that they were aliens and strangers on earth. People who say such things show that they are looking for a country of their own.*
> (Hebrews 11:13-14)

God created a big world filled with all kinds of people. One reason I like living in Las Vegas is because it is so culturally diverse. Other places I have lived, the people all want to be alike. They look the same, talk the same, and think the same. In Las Vegas, people are different, and they celebrate their differences.

One way you can tell that people are different, is by the way they talk. By listening to an accent, you can often tell whether someone is from the Midwest, the Southeast, or outside of the United States. What about you? Can people tell where you are from by the way you talk? More importantly, can people tell that you are a Christian by the words that come from your mouth?

In chapter 13, you learned that God has called you to live in such a way that you counter the culture. You are to be different than the world. This begs the obvious question, "What makes a Christian different?" The answer is simple: the Bible. People of the world live according to their own desires, but the people of God live according to the Word of God.

Allow the Bible to be your compass and your guide. Make all decisions based on what the Word of God says. When you live your life according to the Bible's principles, you will not blend in with the pack. Your values will stand in stark contrast to the world, and you will feel like you are a stranger or alien on the earth.

The Bible

The Bible is God's divine revelation to humanity. He gave His Word to make His name and His will known to the world. It is comprised of 66 books, which were written during a time span of nearly two thousand years by more than forty different writers.

The Bible provides a clear and concise message because it comes directly from God Himself. 2 Timothy 3:16 says that all Scripture is God-breathed, which means God was in control of the writing. 2 Peter 1:21 takes this a step further by explaining that the men who wrote the Bible spoke from God, as they were carried along by the Holy Spirit. Because God inspired the Bible, it is inerrant (without mistake).

God's Word is Truth (see John 17:17). You are incapable of knowing God's Truth on your own because His thoughts are not your thoughts, and His ways are not your ways (see Isaiah 55:8). God did not want you to wonder about His standards, so He revealed them in His Word. The Bible is meant to be the authority manual for your life. It is filled with instructions on how to live by faith.

Study The Bible To Become Spiritually Mature

In his book *Transforming Discipleship*, Greg Ogden said, "Christians in general are ignorant of its [the Bible's] content and hold convictions that are contrary to its clear and central teaching."[1] God did not give His Word so it can sit on your bookshelf or be attractively displayed on your coffee table. Scripture can only guide you if you know what it says.

In other words, you need to study the Bible. But do not be content with mere head knowledge. In Colossians 3:16, it says to let the Word dwell in you, and Psalm 119:11 says to hide God's Word in your heart. You receive God's Word in your head. You process God's Word in your heart. But you live God's Word in your life. As you study the Bible, may it move from your head, to your heart, to your life!

Peter said to crave pure spiritual milk (see 1 Peter 2:2). That means to crave the Word of God. The word "crave" means to desire strongly. It makes me think of wanting something so badly, that I feel I must have it right now! Some people desperately need a nicotine, sugar, chocolate or caffeine fix. Peter said a Christian should crave, or strongly desire, or desperately need God's Word. When you crave the Bible, you desire to know everything that it says. Be sure, however, that you crave only pure milk. Pure spiritual milk has not been watered down to make it user friendly for today's culture. Truth is absolute and never changes. It is just as relevant today as it was 2,000 years ago.

God wants you to grow and mature in your faith. The Word is needed if you are to grow. Only when you actively get into the Word, will you mature as you should, and your desire to live by faith will increase as well. Start out simple. Learn the basic doctrines, and move on from there.

As you study, you will learn to apply the truths of the Bible to your daily life. The Bible is the standard to which everything should be compared. Live your life and base all of your decisions on what God's Word says.

Commit To Stand Upon God's Word

Most people no longer accept that there is absolute truth. This is true even among Christians! You live in a time when truth has become relative. What is right for you may not be what is right for me, and what is right for me may not be what is right for you.

This creates an environment of chaos because nothing is right or wrong. Everything is relative. Truth is however you perceive it. There is no standard. As a result, most people do not know what they believe. If you do not know what you believe, you cannot take a stand for anything, and this leaves you very vulnerable to Satan's attacks. It is true what they say, "If you stand for nothing, you'll fall for everything."

But if you know what you believe and what you stand for, you can handle whatever the world throws at you. Jesus was tempted three times by Satan at the start of His ministry. Each time Jesus was tempted, He responded with Scripture. Jesus knew that He did not live on bread alone, but on every word that comes from the mouth of God (see Matthew 4:4). Jesus, the Son of the living God, depended on the Word of God while a resident of this world. If Jesus felt it was important to know God's Word, so should you.

Live By Faith In The Word Of God

If you want to live as a stranger or an alien in the world, you must take a stand to live your life according to God's absolute Truth—the Bible. Know what the Bible says about the issues that affect your life. Build your life upon its teachings. Make a commitment to stand upon God's Word. This will put you in stark contrast to the world, which is just what God desires.

In closing, I'd like to share with you a poem, which so aptly describes the world today.

"Side By Side"

They lie on the table side by side,
The Holy Bible and the TV guide.
One is well worn and cherished with pride,
No, not the Bible…but the TV guide.

One is used daily to help folks decide,
No, not the Bible…but the TV guide.
As the pages are turned, what shall they see?
Oh, what does it matter, turn on the TV.

Then confusion reigns, they can't all agree,
On what they should watch on the old TV.
So they open the book in which they confide,
No, not the Bible…but the TV guide.

The Word of God is seldom read,
Maybe a verse as they fall into bed.
Exhausted, sleepy and tired as can be,
Not from reading the Bible…from watching TV.
So then back to the table side by side,
Lie the Holy Bible and the TV guide.
No time made for prayer, no time for God's Word,
The plan of Salvation is seldom heard.
But forgiveness of sin, so full and free,
Is found in the Bible…not on TV.

(©Shawnee Kellie—Used With Permission)

Strengthen Your Faith

Christians are supposed to make their decisions based on what the Word of God says. How do non-believers make their decisions and determine their values?

According to 2 Timothy 3:16, what makes the Bible different from any other book?

Read 1 Peter 2:2. Explain what it means to crave pure spiritual milk.

Describe an area in your life, which you have not placed under the authority of God's Word.

15

NEVER LOOK BACK

If they had been thinking of the country they had left, they would have had opportunity to return. Instead, they were longing for a better country—a heavenly one. Therefore God is not ashamed to be called their God, for he has prepared a city for them.
(Hebrews 11:15-16)

Satchel Paige was one of the greatest baseball players of all time. He played most of his career in the old Negro leagues, because at that time black athletes were not allowed in major league baseball. When Jackie Robinson broke the color barrier, Satchel Paige was signed by the Cleveland Indians, and led them to a World Series. After pitching his team to a victory, he was interviewed by a mass of reporters. They drilled him with questions about the trials and obstacles he faced as a black athlete. When asked how he managed to keep going through it all, Satchel Paige smiled to the cameras and said, "I never looked back. I never looked back."

<u>Faith Looks Forward</u>

When Abraham began his journey of faith, he did not think about his past or what he left behind. If he had dwelt on the past, chances are, he would have given up on his journey and returned home. But Abraham chose to live by faith. He focused on what God had in store for him in the future. Remember, faith deals with future things, which are promised by God. Abraham continued on his journey because he longed for a better country, a heavenly one.

Paul wrote about a similar experience. In Philippians 3:13-14, he likened the journey of faith to an athletic race.

> Brothers, I do not consider myself yet to have taken hold of it. But one thing I do: Forgetting what is behind and straining toward what is ahead, I press on toward the goal to win the prize for which God has called me heavenward in Christ Jesus.

The race Paul is describing here is not a fifty-yard sprint. It is more like a marathon. So it is with life. As you run the race of life, there will be times when you run with ease and there will be times that you struggle. On your journey of faith, you can expect good times and bad, mountaintops and valleys. These two verses show three things you must do if you desire to succeed on your journey of faith.

Forget The Past

In order to succeed, Paul had to forget his "past." He could not dwell on the fact that he had been an enemy of the church. He had to forget that he had persecuted Christians and was present at the stoning of Stephen. Talk about skeletons in the closet. Paul understood that he was starting a new chapter in his life, and that to be successful, he must forget the bad things in his past.

What about you? Is something in your past weighing you down and preventing you from succeeding in your Christian life? Is there some sin that continues to haunt you? Maybe there is a series of poor choices you can't seem to get out of your mind, or maybe you have a relationship that needs to be repaired. Friends, I don't know what a sinner you are, but I know what a Savior He is. If God can forgive Paul and use him as a missionary, God can forgive you and use you in His kingdom. But if you want to succeed, you must receive God's forgiveness and forget the bad things in your past.

Paul also had to forget the good things in his past. He is recognized as the greatest missionary in the early church. Paul personally started more churches and led more people to Christ than any of his contemporaries. His boldness, his untiring faith, and his impact on the Gentiles for the kingdom of God, was unequaled among his peers. But Paul said, "I must forget the past." He was not willing to rest on past accomplishments…and neither should you.

Successful Christians never rest on their past accomplishments. God isn't interested in what you did for Him ten years ago. God wants to know what you are doing for Him today! When you talk about your faith and have to go back one year, two years or ten years, to find something you have done for God, you are living in the past. This Scripture serves as a reminder to put the past behind you and live for God today.

The beautiful part about the journey of faith is that when you hop onboard, you leave your baggage behind. Past sins, past failures, even past successes, are not allowed. You will be provided with all you need. That is why it is a journey of "faith." You have to believe that God will provide for all of your needs. The journey of faith is a great opportunity for a new beginning in life. But it all begins when you let go of the past, take that giant step of faith, and never look back. Never look back.

Look Forward

Abraham never thought about what he left behind (see Hebrews 11:15). He was totally focused on what was ahead. Paul lived the same way. In Philippians 3:13, Paul said he was "straining" toward what was ahead. In this verse Paul wanted you to visualize a runner using every muscle, every ounce of energy to cross the finish line and win the race. He described giving 110%; never looking back because if he looked back, he may lose the race. As a Christian on the journey of faith, you must know what your goal is and keep straining to reach that goal.

Press On

I cannot imagine the trials, setbacks, and obstacles that Satchel Paige had to endure on his journey to major league baseball. Most of his contemporaries quit along the way, but not Satchel Paige. He pressed on despite trial and adversity. So did Abraham and Paul. Abraham lived during a time of severe famine. He also experienced the kidnapping of a close relative, and turmoil in his family life. Paul was beaten and thrown into jail. In fact, Paul wrote Philippians while he was sitting in a prison cell. Yet they pressed on toward the goal to win the prize for which God had called them heavenward in Christ Jesus.

What about you? How do you respond when pressures come, and temptations arise? Do you stand firm in your faith and press on, or do you give in to the pressures of the world? As you run your race called the journey of faith, you can learn much from Abraham and Paul. Follow their example and forget the past, look forward to what lies ahead, and press on toward the goal.

Just as Abraham never looked back, neither should you. Abraham never thought about the place he left because it paled in comparison to where he was going. Faith opened the way for Abraham to live in a better country—heaven. And the same is true for you

Strengthen Your Faith

How is the journey of faith like a marathon?

According to Philippians 3:13-14, what three things must you do to be successful on your journey of faith?

What are some things in your past, which hold you down and prevent you from reaching your potential as a Christian?

Take time to confess your sins to God. By faith, receive God's complete forgiveness. Make a commitment to follow Jesus and never look back!

16

ASSURANCE OF SALVATION

If they had been thinking of the country they had left, they would have had opportunity to return. Instead, they were longing for a better country—a heavenly one. Therefore God is not ashamed to be called their God, for he has prepared a city for them.
(Hebrews 11:15-16)

    I'll never forget the time my wife and I purchased our first home. It was the biggest financial decision we had ever made. As we sat in the attorney's office, we were amazed at how many pages we had to sign. We felt as if we were signing our life away to the bank. These pages were part of a contract between the bank and our family. The bank agreed to loan us the money to purchase our home. Lisa and I agreed to repay the money plus interest.

    Most people are familiar with contracts. A contract is a legal document, which specifies the responsibilities of each party involved in an agreement. A contract can be broken if one of the parties fails to keep their end of the agreement, or if a cunning lawyer finds a loophole. For this reason, you will sometimes hear it said that a contract is not worth the paper it is written on.

The Assurance Of Salvation

Thankfully, when you put your trust in Christ for salvation, you do more than sign a contract. You enter into a binding relationship with God, whereby He adopts you as His very own child. Once you become a part of God's family, nothing can sever those ties. There is a place reserved for you in heaven. This is called the assurance of salvation.

One way I like to explain the assurance of salvation is by describing my relationship with one of my children. My older son's name is Stephen. When Lisa and I discovered we were going to have a child, we knew it would forever change our lives. After Stephen's birth, I held him in my arms and thought, "This is my son. Nothing will ever change this fact. God has given me a son, and from this moment forward, I will always be his father."

As Stephen reaches adulthood, he must make his own choices about how he will live, where he will live, and with whom (not with us!). If Stephen so chooses, he can leave home, move to New York City, and never call me again. He can reject me, claim he doesn't know me, and deny he has any family at all. It is possible that he could leave home and I won't hear from him for thirty years. But even thirty years later, if you ask me whether I have a son, I will say, "Yes I do. His name is Stephen. He is my son and I am his father." He may leave. He may stop loving me. But I will never stop loving him because he is my son and I am his father. Nothing can ever change that.

Choosing How To Live

As you grow toward adulthood in your Christian life, God allows you the freedom to decide how you will live. You can decide to live your life by faith, or you can try to live your life in your own power. But remember, God only makes His power available to those who live by faith (see 1 Peter 1:5). Although you have the freedom to walk away from your life of faith, you can never walk away from your salvation. Your salvation is secure for all eternity.

The statement "your salvation is secure for all eternity" brings to mind two common questions about Christianity. 1. How can I know if I am going to heaven? 2. Is it possible to lose my place in heaven? The answers to these questions are important building blocks of your faith and are clearly explained in Scripture.

How To Know If You Are Going To Heaven

How can you know if you are going to heaven? The Bible gives a very clear answer to this question. It is through faith in Jesus that you receive eternal life in heaven. The Bible says, "For God so loved the world that he gave his one and only Son, that whoever believes in him shall not perish but have eternal life" (John 3:16). Faith in Jesus is the *only* way to the Father (see John 14:6).

You need to fully understand that Jesus died on the cross in *your* place. He paid the price for *your* sins when He died, and showed His victory over *your* death when He rose from the dead three days later. When you believe these facts, and trust Jesus enough to give Him your life, you are saved. Once you are saved, you have reserved your spot in heaven.

But what if you do not feel saved? The issue is not how you feel. Do not trust your feelings. They can change as rapidly as the weather. Some people feel there must be something more they have to do. There is nothing you can do to earn your salvation, and nothing you must do to keep from losing it. When Jesus died on the cross, He said, "It is finished" (see John

19:30). Salvation is by grace through faith alone (see Ephesians 2:8-9).

Can You Lose Your Place In Heaven?

Is it possible to lose your place in heaven? No! God created you and fully understands that it is human nature for you to crave security. He wants you to fully understand that you are His for all eternity. You cannot lose your salvation. The saying, "Once saved, always saved" is true. Jesus promised He would not lose anyone given to Him (see John 6:39). When you are saved, you place your eternal future into Jesus' hands. The Bible says that no one can snatch you out of His hands (see John 10:28).

Ephesians 1:13b-14 says, "Having believed, you were marked in him with a seal, the promised Holy Spirit, who is a deposit guaranteeing our inheritance until the redemption of those who are God's possession." The Holy Spirit comes into you and indwells you at the time of your salvation. He guarantees your salvation and also what is to come. The Holy Spirit is God's seal of eternal ownership. Just like a tattoo permanently marks your skin, the Holy Spirit is a permanent mark that shows you belong to Jesus. You belong to God for all eternity.

Once you belong to Christ, it is impossible to be separated from Him. Romans 8:38-39 says, "For I am convinced that neither death nor life, neither angels nor demons, neither the present *nor the future*, nor any powers, neither height nor depth, nor *anything else in all creation*, will be able to separate us from the love of God that is in Christ Jesus our Lord" (emphasis added). This is a powerful promise. *Nothing* can separate you.

You may think that sounds too good to be true and wonder what will happen if you backslide and no longer walk by faith. Or even worse, what if you decide you no longer want to be saved? Nothing that happens in the future can take you away from Christ; not even a decision you make, because you are part of the "anything else" in all creation.

Choose To Live By Faith

I feel a great sense of peace because of the assurance of my salvation. It is such a relief to know I don't have to spend my days wondering where I will end up when I die. I know that heaven is my eternal destination.

Studying these heroes can help you keep your eyes focused on the walk of faith. These people did not look back to their old life. They had forward-looking faith. The secret to forward-looking faith is to fix your eyes on Jesus, the author and perfecter of your faith (see Hebrews 12:2). When you focus your eyes of faith on Jesus, you will begin to experience the sense of security, which comes from knowing you belong to Him forever.

Strengthen Your Faith

What is the difference between a contract and a binding personal relationship?

Read 1 John 5:12-13. What do these verses teach about the assurance of salvation?

Think about a time in your life when you didn't feel saved. What caused you to have these feelings? What did you do about them?

Take time this week to share this lesson with a friend who may be struggling with the issue of assurance.

17

THE TESTING OF OUR FAITH

By faith Abraham, when God tested him, offered Isaac as a sacrifice. He who had received the promises was about to sacrifice his one and only son, even though God had said to him, "It is through Isaac that your offspring will be reckoned." Abraham reasoned that God could raise the dead, and figuratively speaking, he did receive Isaac back from death.
(Hebrews 11:17-19)

I believe that life is a lot like a golf course. A golf course consists of beautiful fairways, smooth greens, and sand traps. The same is true in life. You will have times in your life when you experience beautiful fairways and smooth greens. At other times, you will find yourself mired in the sand trap of tough times.

In golf, a sand trap is designed to test your ability. How you respond to the sand trap is a good indicator of your skill level. In the same way, how you respond to the tests of life reveals the genuineness of your faith. It is easy to portray faith while living on the beautiful fairways and smooth greens. But what about when you find yourself in the sand trap of tough times?

The Story—Abraham Asked To Sacrifice Isaac

God tested Abraham. He told him to take his son, Isaac, to Mt. Moriah, and sacrifice him. Abraham's two servants did not go with them to their final destination. "He said to his servants, 'Stay here with the donkey while I and the boy go over there. We will worship and then we will come back to you'" (Genesis 22:5).

As they continued on, Isaac asked Abraham where the lamb was for the burnt offering. Abraham told Isaac that God would provide the lamb. When they reached their destination, Abraham bound Isaac and placed him on the altar he had built. As Abraham reached for the knife to kill Isaac, the angel of the Lord stopped him. "Do not lay a hand on the boy," he said. "Do not do anything to him. Now I know that you fear God, because you have not withheld from me your son, your only son" (Genesis 22:12). A ram was trapped in a nearby thicket, and Abraham sacrificed the lamb to God. Abraham named the place "The LORD Will Provide." Because of his obedience, God promised Abraham abundant blessings.

What Is A Test/Trial?

God asked Abraham to do the unthinkable—to sacrifice his beloved son, Isaac. Isaac was Abraham's miracle child, born in his old age. It was Isaac's descendants that God promised would be made into a great nation that would bless the entire world (see Genesis 21:12). Isaac was central to the fulfillment of God's promise. Why would God want him sacrificed?

God was testing Abraham. This test required Abraham to prove that he truly loved God more than anyone or anything. Its purpose was not to prove to God that Abraham loved Him more than anything else. God is omniscient (all-knowing). He already knew Abraham would pass the test. The test was designed to show *Abraham* the extent of his faith.

What is a test of faith? Bruce Wilkinson, in his book *Secrets of the Vine*, provides a definition, which explains Abraham's situation very well. He said, "Tests of faith are various trials and hardships that invite you to surrender something of great value to God *even when you have every right not to.*"[1]

A test is different than a temptation. A test is from God and is designed to help you grow in your faith. A temptation is from Satan and its purpose is to defeat you spiritually, ultimately causing your faith to weaken. Every negative circumstance in your life is not a test. Be careful not to confuse the negative consequences of a poor decision with a test.

A given situation can be both a test and a temptation, with God using it to increase your faith, while Satan tries to derail it. There are two important points to bring out regarding Satan. First, Satan cannot bring anything into your life unless God allows it. Satan needs God's permission (see Job 1; Luke 22:31-32), because God is sovereign (in control). Second, God already knows the outcome of the test, and Satan does not. As powerful as Satan is, he is not God. Satan is a created being. He does not have foreknowledge of how you will respond to a test. Only God truly knows what the future holds.

> The purpose of a test is to increase or mature your faith.

> Consider it pure joy, my brothers, whenever you face trials of many kinds, because you know that the testing of your faith develops perseverance. Perseverance must finish its work so that you may be mature and complete, not lacking anything. (James 1:2-4)

The phrase "trials of many kinds" indicates you will face

numerous tests during your life. "Whenever" show that you cannot escape trials. If it were possible to avoid trials, the verse would say, "*If* you face trials...." The Amplified Bible uses the word "encounter" instead of "face." To "encounter" explains that you are not the cause of the trouble.

Remember, the purpose of a test is to strengthen your faith and take it to the next level. Each test stretches you to your limit, and your limit increases each time you pass. This means your next test will push you further than the previous one, which was more difficult than the test before that. Do not allow this fact to frighten you. God promises He will not allow a circumstance, which is beyond what you can bear (see 1 Corinthians 10:13).

Abraham's Obedience When Tested

When God requested that Isaac be sacrificed, Abraham could have responded in several ways. First, Abraham could have said, "NO!" Second, he could have stalled. Abraham could have thought, "Surely I misunderstood God. There is no way that God wants me to kill my own son." Most people would fall into one of these two categories. There was a third option available to Abraham—he could say yes.

This is the option that Abraham chose. It is the way of obedience. Abraham said, "Yes, I am willing to do whatever God requires." He prepared to sacrifice Isaac, and God intervened—but not until the last possible second. God did not stop the sacrifice until Abraham was about to use the knife to kill his son (see Genesis 22:10-11).

Abraham's response to God was the same as Noah's. Abraham obeyed God. He acted on what he believed. Abraham obeyed because he feared God (see Genesis 22:12). His obedience demonstrated his faith. Abraham was willing to give God that which was most precious to him, his beloved son, Isaac. Abraham showed his willingness to give everything to God (see Matthew 16:24; Romans 12:1). This was visible proof of his faith. Abraham's test helped mature his faith. When he returned from Mt. Moriah, his faith was stronger than when he started out for the sacrifice.

God's Provision

A ram was trapped in a nearby thicket, and Abraham sacrificed the lamb to God. The ram was probably there all along, because God never intended for Abraham to go through with the sacrifice of Isaac. After Abraham sacrificed the ram, he named the place "The Lord Will Provide." God has many names, and He uses them to reveal His character and His attributes. In Genesis 22:14, it is revealed that God is Jehovah Jireh—The Lord Who Provides.

Just as God had a ram ready for Abraham, He will provide for you as well. But you will not see God's provision until you have obeyed. Abraham did not see the ram until he obeyed and was willing to give everything to God, regardless of the cost. The same holds true for you. God will not reveal all of His plans for you. He wants you to trust Him. God wants you to keep your eyes on Him. When you obey and are willing to give it all to God, you will pass the test, and your faith will soar to new levels. Keep your eyes of faith focused on God during a test. He will provide.

Strengthen Your Faith

What is the difference between a test and a temptation?

According to James 1:2-4, what is the purpose of a test or a trial?

Describe a time in your life when a test caused your faith to increase.

18

WHEN GOD DOESN'T MAKE SENSE

> *By faith Abraham, when God tested him, offered Isaac as a sacrifice. He who had received the promises was about to sacrifice his one and only son, even though God had said to him, "It is through Isaac that your offspring will be reckoned." Abraham reasoned that God could raise the dead, and figuratively speaking, he did receive Isaac back from death.*
> (Hebrews 11:17-19)

Have you ever done something, even though it didn't make any sense? A few years ago, I walked to my car in a mall parking lot only to find someone had dented my car door. Because the dent was in a very obvious spot, I knew my wife would want the car repaired. I took my car to the local body shop and asked for an estimate. The manager told me he could repair the dent in my car for $750. I decided to think about it for a while.

A few days later, when I was filling my car up with gas, the station owner asked me about the dent in my door. I explained what happened, and then asked him what he thought about the quote of $750. He told me he thought the price seemed high. We talked a little more and then he asked me if I would go to the hardware store and buy him a plunger. I said, "I don't understand. Why in the world do you want me to buy you a plunger?" He told me I didn't need to understand, I just needed to get a plunger.

I had no idea why he wanted the plunger, but I decided to do exactly as he said. When I returned with the plunger, he put it on the door of my car and popped out the dent in fifteen seconds. I asked him how much I owed for the repairs. He smiled and said, "I sure could use a new plunger." I gave him the plunger and saved $745.

Abraham Trusted God

I think Abraham was very confused when God told him to take his son, Isaac, to Mt. Moriah, and sacrifice him. Remember, God had already explained that His promise to make Abraham into a great nation would be fulfilled through Isaac (see Genesis 21:12). Although it didn't make sense, Abraham was obedient and did exactly as God instructed. It was only after Abraham demonstrated complete obedience that God revealed His plan.

God knew all along what He was going to do, but Abraham didn't. God's plan was for Abraham to sacrifice a ram, which was trapped in a nearby thicket. But God did not reveal the ram to Abraham until he obeyed God and followed His instructions. Abraham first needed to demonstrate that he trusted God, even when it made no sense. Only then did Abraham see the ram God provided.

Jesus Raised Lazarus From The Dead

The Bible is filled with stories of people who trusted God, even when it made no sense. One of my favorites is about a brother and two sisters who were part of Jesus' inner circle. Their names were Lazarus, Mary, and Martha. At one point, Lazarus became very ill. "So the sisters sent word to Jesus, 'Lord, the one you love is sick'" (John 11:3). The sisters believed Jesus would drop what He was doing, and rush to the aid of His dear friend. "Yet when he [Jesus] heard that Lazarus was sick, he stayed where he was two more days" (John 11:6). Lazarus died. His sisters wrapped him in burial clothes and laid him in a tomb. Four days later, Jesus arrived in Bethany. Mary and Martha wondered why Jesus had not come sooner. They felt abandoned in their hour of need. Their reaction is certainly understandable. The women said, "Lord, if you had been here, my brother would not have died" (see John 11:21, 32). Look at what transpired next.

> Jesus, once more deeply moved, came to the tomb. It was a cave with a stone laid across the entrance. "Take away the stone," he said. "But, Lord," said Martha, the sister of the dead man, "by this time there is a bad odor, for he has been there four days." (John 11:38-39)

Jesus' command made no sense. Why did He want the stone rolled away? Didn't Jesus have the power to move the stone Himself? Of course He did. Jesus wanted Mary and Martha to demonstrate their faith. The sisters obeyed Jesus, even though His request did not make sense to them. They took away the stone blocking the entrance to Lazarus' tomb. Jesus prayed to God, then called out in a loud voice,

> "Lazarus, come out!" The dead man came out, his hands and feet wrapped with strips of linen, and a cloth around his face. Jesus said to them, "Take off the grave clothes and let him go." (John 11:43b-44)

Mary and Martha didn't understand why Jesus delayed. It made no sense to them. However, they trusted Jesus. Because they trusted Jesus, they obeyed when He told them to take away the stone. This enabled them to witness a great miracle. Jesus brought their beloved brother, Lazarus, back to life.

Trust God—Even When It Doesn't Make Sense

In all my years as a pastor, I have never come to the point where I completely understand God. In fact, I have come to the conclusion that I will never fully understand God. If I did, He would no longer be God. Isaiah 55:8-9 says,

> "For my thoughts are not your thoughts, neither are your ways my ways," declares the LORD. "As the heavens are higher than the earth, so are my ways higher than your ways and my thoughts than your thoughts."

When God tells you to do something that doesn't make sense, I encourage you not to rely on your own understanding. Instead, trust and rely on God. Someone once told me, "Let God be God." It is not His duty to explain His ways. It is your duty to obey Him and follow His instructions. You do not need to understand why. You just need to understand Who. If God says it, that should settle it, even if it doesn't make sense. Your goal, on the journey of faith, is to trust God, even when it doesn't make sense.

What Is Trust?

The *Life Application Study Bible* defines trust as "to place one's confidence in; to hope."[1] So to trust God is to place your full confidence in Him. You learn to trust God as you spend time with Him. Trust starts with knowing God. To know God is to be sure of His character and His attributes. Once you know and understand who God is, you become confident He will keep His promises. You believe Him. You trust Him. This causes your faith to grow.

Trust God With Your Life

Proverbs 3:5-6 is a very popular Bible verse. It says,

> Trust in the LORD with all your heart and lean not on your own understanding; in all your ways acknowledge him, and he will make your paths straight.

The NIV translation says, "Do not lean on your own understanding." The word "lean" implies resting your weight on something. Think of it as resting the weight of your decisions or difficulties on God. Trust Him completely in everything you do.

When you catch yourself saying, "I think I should…," you are relying on your understanding, and are headed for trouble. Immediately turn it over to God. Trust Him. Here is how I paraphrase these verses: Place your full confidence in God; do not rely on yourself. Put Him first and He will show you what to do.

Develop Trust And Intimacy With God

Remember, to trust God is to place your full confidence in Him. Now, relate this to your personal life. Who are the people in whom you have complete confidence? Whom do you trust? Maybe it is your spouse, your parents, or perhaps, a lifelong friend? These people all have one thing in common with you: an intimate relationship. You spend time together, and have been through the process of getting to know one another.

Did you know that God desires to have a close personal relationship with you? God wants you to know Him very well, because when you know Him, you will believe what He says. And when you believe God, you will trust Him. And like Abraham, if you trust Him, you will obey Him. Abraham was called God's friend (see James 2:23). That is such an honor. God wants to be your friend as well. Just as your earthly friendships require intimacy and trust to flourish, so does your relationship with God. Make it the goal of your life to know and trust God. When you have true friendship with God, you will trust Him, even when it doesn't make sense.

Strengthen Your Faith

God told Abraham to sacrifice Isaac. Describe how you would react to such a command.

Who is someone you trust completely? How did you develop such a high level of trust with this person?

Meditate on Proverbs 3:5-6. Apply these verses to a major decision you need to make.

19

MIRACLES AND FAITH

By faith Abraham, when God tested him, offered Isaac as a sacrifice. He who had received the promises was about to sacrifice his one and only son, even though God had said to him, "It is through Isaac that your offspring will be reckoned." Abraham reasoned that God could raise the dead, and figuratively speaking, he did receive Isaac back from death.
(Hebrews 11:17-19)

Do you believe in miracles? A couple of years ago, I saw a movie called *Miracle*. The movie chronicled the story of how the US hockey team won the gold medal at the 1980 Olympics. Hockey fans will tell you it was a miracle that the United States beat the Russians, and won the gold medal that year. If you are not a hockey fan or can't remember back to 1980, you might recall when the Boston Red Sox beat the New York Yankees in the American League Championship Series of 2004. Boston was down three games to zero in a best of seven series. The Yankees were within one out of winning it all. But the Red Sox came back, and won the series in one of the biggest upsets in sports history.

When I talk about miracles, forgive me if I want to go a little deeper than a hockey or baseball game. Although I do believe God is concerned with all areas of your life, I think that

His greatest miracles are the ones He does in you, not around you. My simple definition of a miracle is something that happens in your life, which cannot be explained apart from the power and sovereignty of God.

The Bible is filled with miraculous stories. You may remember that God parted the Red Sea, allowing the Israelites to cross on dry ground. God also caused the walls of Jericho to collapse, enabling the Israelites to enter and take the highly fortified city. David, a mere shepherd boy, killed the giant Goliath with a simple slingshot. Jesus also performed many miracles while He walked the earth. He turned water into wine, gave sight to the blind, helped the lame to walk and the mute to talk. These are just a few of the many miracles revealed in God's Word.

You have undoubtedly witnessed modern miracles. A church member, who was in a coma for six weeks, told me it is a miracle that she's alive today. I know a heart attack victim who considers himself a walking miracle. Maybe you know someone who was dying of cancer and the cancer disappeared, or a baby that was not supposed to live but miraculously recovered. The world is filled with miracles. God is the God of miracles.

<u>Isaac's Birth Was A Miracle</u>

The birth of Isaac was truly a miracle of God. Remember, Abraham was one hundred years old and Sarah was ninety. They were well beyond childbearing years, yet God told Sarah that she would give birth to a son. Do you remember how Sarah responded to the news? She laughed. Sarah laughed because she knew that at ninety years of age it was impossible to have a child. There was no way Abraham and Sarah could explain Isaac's birth apart from the power and sovereignty of God. I believe God intentionally waited until Abraham and Sarah were in their twilight years so that there would be no doubt in their minds that Isaac's birth was a miracle.

Although Sarah laughed, Abraham trusted God implicitly because he had seen God work in the past. Previously, Abraham obeyed God and left Ur for the place God would show him. God blessed Abraham's faith and obedience with the miraculous birth of a son in his old age.

What Are Miracles?

The *Life Application Study Bible* defines a miracle as a "divine act unexplainable by the laws of nature."[1] In other words, a miracle is an act, which can only be explained by God's power. When a miracle happens, it is as if God shines a huge spotlight on His power. Each time God does the impossible, He demonstrates to the world that with God all things are possible (see Matthew 19:26). God does not perform a miracle just for kicks. There is a purpose behind each miracle, and a miracle will not happen without faith (see Matthew 13:58).

Isaac's birth is a wonderful example of a miracle for two reasons. First, his birth accomplished the impossible. He was conceived to two very senior adults, which demonstrated God's power. The experience showed Abraham that God had the ability to give life to a body which was as good as dead reproductively. Second, there was purpose behind Isaac's birth, because it was through Isaac that God would make a great nation (see Genesis 21:12).

God Used A Miracle To Prepare Abraham For His Test

Sometimes God uses a miracle to strengthen your faith. When God performs a miracle in your life, it enables you to see

His power first hand. It provides an opportunity for God to intervene and help, to show that He cares. In the future, when you experience hard times, you can think back to that miracle and be reminded of how God helped you in the past.

God used the miracle of Isaac's birth to help prepare Abraham for the ultimate test of his faith: to sacrifice his son (see Genesis 22:1-2). Abraham believed God would keep His promise to make Isaac's descendants into a great nation. He also knew, from previous experience, that God had the power to back it up. Abraham believed God was able to do whatever was necessary to keep His word, even if that meant raising the dead (see Hebrews 11:19).

Because Abraham had witnessed Isaac's miraculous birth, He knew that God had the power to do anything. So Abraham assumed that if he killed Isaac, God would somehow bring his son back to life. He believed Isaac's death would only be temporary. Abraham did not know how God would restore life to Isaac, but He believed with all of his heart that God would raise him from the dead. It is equally impressive to note that Abraham believed in the resurrection of the dead before God ever revealed the concept.

You have already learned through this study of Hebrews 11 that faith has visible action to back it up. Abraham demonstrated his faith when he said to his servants that *they* would both return from the sacrifice (see Genesis 22:5). Abraham's faith and actions worked together (see James 2:22). He clearly showed that he believed God would keep His promise.

<u>Abraham's Faith Provided Confidence</u>

Abraham was tested by God and passed with flying colors. He obeyed God, no matter what the cost. He was able to do this because he trusted God. Abraham had experienced God in the past. This strengthened his faith and prepared him for the future. His faith gave him confidence at a crucial time in his life.

Faith can do the same for you. Take the time to deepen your relationship with God, and strengthen your faith. When you enter a time of testing, your faith will provide the confidence you need to persevere. As you persevere, your faith will mature (see James 1:4). When the test is over you will find yourself at the next level in your journey of faith.

Jesus' Birth—God's Ultimate Miracle For His Ultimate Plan

Jesus was miraculously conceived. Jesus' mother was a virgin. He was conceived by the power of the Holy Spirit. The miracle of Jesus' birth was for God's ultimate purpose—the salvation of the world. Jesus was born to save His people from their sins. He was literally born to die.

Hebrews 11:19 says that Abraham "figuratively" received Isaac back from death. Abraham planned to kill his son, but Isaac was never actually sacrificed. Instead, God provided a substitute. There was a ram trapped in a thicket, which Abraham sacrificed in Isaac's place (see Genesis 22:13).

Isaac's figurative death foreshadowed what would happen to Jesus. However, Jesus' death was not figurative. He literally died and came back to life. Just as a ram was substituted for Isaac, Jesus is your substitute. Jesus was sacrificed for your sin. Jesus is the Lamb of God that takes away the sin of the world (see John 1:29). He was the final blood sacrifice (see Hebrews 9:26), and was sent as an atoning sacrifice for your sins (see 1 John 4:10). He paid the ultimate price for your sins.

Strengthen Your Faith

Write out your own definition of a miracle.

What would you say is the purpose of miracles?

God is the God of miracles. Which of His miracles do you consider to be the greatest? Why?

Make a list of the miracles you have experienced in your life, and thank God for them.

20

HOW TO BLESS YOUR CHILDREN

By faith Isaac blessed Jacob and Esau in regard to their future.
(Hebrews 11:20)

One of the most popular Christian books of our generation is *The Blessing*, by Gary Smalley and John Trent. In this book the authors discuss the importance of blessing your children. As a Christian parent, one of the most important things you can do is to "bless" your children or pass along your faith to them. To bless your children means to touch them, affirm them, place a high value on them, and let them know that God has great plans for their lives. Far to often parents burden their children instead of blessing them.

My mom had great dreams and aspirations for me. She truly believed in me and made it a point to tell me that time and time again. From a very early age, she instilled in me the belief that I could be anything I wanted to be. Somewhere along the way, I began to believe it myself. Because my mother was politically active, she thought I would one day go into politics.

I graduated from college with a degree in Accounting and accepted a position with a CPA firm. My mom was happy. She thought her only son was a success. She was proud of what I had achieved and where I was headed in life. What she didn't know was that God had other plans for me. God wanted me to leave the business world and become a pastor. When I made the decision to quit my job and go to seminary, I knew I had to tell my mother. I did not look forward to this because I knew that she would be crushed by the news.

I tried to plan the setting for this announcement as wisely as possible. I decided to invite her to come for a weekend visit. After a nice dinner I told her it would be a good idea if she sat down because I had something very important to share with her. I said, "Mom, I am not going to be a politician. I am not going to be a lawyer. I am not even going to be an accountant. I want you to know that I have resigned my position at the firm because I am going to be a pastor!"

As I looked at her face I can honestly say that she was speechless. This news blindsided her in such a way that I thought she was going to faint. She remained silent as she processed it all. After what seemed like an eternity, she spoke, and I'll never forget her words for as long as I live. She placed her hands on my shoulders, looked me in the eyes and said, "And you'll be the best pastor in the whole world!"

At that moment, I knew I had the blessing of my mom and that I could follow God's call on my life with her total support. She demonstrated what Smalley and Trent discussed in their book. My mother placed her hands upon me, and spoke words of approval. She valued me, believed in me, and painted a picture of how God would use me in a special way as a pastor. I thank God today that I received a blessing from my mother.

Background On Jacob And Esau

When Isaac was forty years old, he married Rebekah. Isaac prayed to God because Rebekah could not have children. God answered his prayer and Rebekah became pregnant with twins. God told Rebekah the twins she was carrying would be two separate nations (the Israelites and the Edomites). One nation would be stronger; the older would serve the younger (see Genesis 25:23).

Esau was born first, and Jacob second. Isaac loved Esau, who was a hunter and outdoorsman. Rebekah loved Jacob, who was a quiet homebody. One day, Esau came home famished. In order to receive some of Jacob's stew, he sold Jacob his birthright. Esau sold his inheritance rights as the oldest son for a single meal (see Hebrews 12:16).

Isaac Blesses Jacob

Isaac called Esau and told him that after Esau prepared him a delicious meal, he would give Esau his blessing. Rebekah overheard their conversation and told Jacob what Isaac had said. Rebekah had Jacob go and kill two young goats, so she could make some food for Isaac. Her intention was for Jacob to take the food to his father and receive the blessing. Rebekah told Jacob to wear a disguise when he took Isaac the meal. Jacob wore Esau's clothes. He also covered his hands and neck with goatskins because Esau was a hairy man and Jacob was smooth-skinned.

Jacob followed his mother's plan. He told his father that he was Esau. Isaac could no longer see and this made it difficult for Isaac to know to whom he was speaking. Isaac touched his son to be sure he really was Esau. After he finished his meal, Isaac blessed Jacob (all the while thinking he was Esau).

> Ah, the smell of my son is like the smell of a field that the LORD has blessed. May God give you of heaven's dew and of earth's richness—an abundance of grain and new wine. May nations serve you and peoples bow down to you. Be lord over your brothers, and may the sons of your mother bow down to you. May those who curse you be cursed and those who bless you be blessed. (Genesis 27:27b-29)

When Esau found out what happened, he cried for his father to bless him as well. His tears could not change anything. Even though Esau wanted to inherit Isaac's blessing, he was rejected (see Hebrews 12:17). Isaac said,

> Your dwelling will be away from the earth's richness, away from the dew of heaven above. You will live by the sword and you will serve your brother. But when you grow restless, you will throw his yoke from off your neck. (Genesis 27:39-40)

Isaac offered Jacob a heart-felt blessing as he left for Paddan Aram to find a wife from among his mother's people. The blessing was as follows:

> May God Almighty bless you and make you fruitful and increase your numbers until you become a community of peoples. May he give you and your descendants the blessing given to Abraham, so that you may take possession of the land where you now live as an alien, the land God gave to Abraham. (Genesis 28:3-4)

The Significance Of The Blessing

When Isaac reached the end of his life, he had not seen the fulfillment of God's promises. Because Isaac believed God, he passed the promised inheritance on to Jacob through his blessing. The blessing was a very important part of family life in the Old Testament. The blessing officially handed the birthright over to the heir. In effect, it transferred the family inheritance. The blessing also provided an opportunity for a father to tell his child about their future.

As you look at the way Isaac blessed Jacob, you can easily

see how Smalley and Trent derived their definition of what it means to "bless" someone. Isaac touched his son on the arms and held him. He spoke words of value and approval. Isaac told Jacob of the bright future and great plans God had for him. It is a beautiful picture of a father passing on his faith to his son. There is nothing more important than passing your faith on to your children.

<u>Bless Your Children</u>

Let me share a final word to parents. Bless your children. When you bless your children, you recognize their importance. It shows that you value them. "I love you for who you are," is an example of a blessing. A blessing is not the same thing as praise. A blessing is encouragement, which is not tied to achievement. Praise commends accomplishment. Praise typically begins with, "You are so wonderful because you did…."

Give your children a positive inheritance by blessing them. Help your children realize that God loves them and that God's love is better than life (see Psalm 63:3). Remind your children that they are wonderfully made by God (see Psalm 139:14), and that He places a high value on them. Make sure they understand that God has special plans for their future (see Jeremiah 29:11). Use a blessing to pass on your faith to the next generation.

Strengthen Your Faith

What does it mean to bless your children?

Describe a time when you received a blessing from someone you admire?

What are some of the benefits associated with blessing your children?

Bless your children today. You'll be glad you did.

21

AN ENCOUNTER WITH GOD

By faith Jacob, when he was dying, blessed each of Joseph's sons, and worshiped as he leaned on the top of his staff.
(Hebrews 11:21)

Worship is the natural response to an encounter with God. I heard a story about an old established church. One Sunday morning, shortly after the service started, a man on the third row stood up during a hymn and shouted, "Hallelujah." Everyone was startled by the man's outburst. Later in the service, when the special music ended, the man yelled out, "Praise God!" Everyone in the church stared at the man. No one had ever exhibited such behavior in this church before. But no one said a word to him.

When the pastor began his sermon, all eyes were on the man in the third row. Every time the pastor quoted the Bible, the man shouted, "Amen!" This happened a half dozen times. It so distracted the congregation that no one heard a word the pastor said. At the conclusion of the service, the pastor asked the head usher to take care of the problem.

The usher approached the man, told him it was inappropriate to speak out in church, and explained proper church behavior. The man listened attentively to everything the usher had to say. When he was finished, the man explained that he felt compelled to speak out because he'd had a personal encounter with

God. To which the usher replied, "Well, you didn't encounter Him here!"

Jacob The Deceiver Did Not Live By Faith

You learned in the previous lesson that Jacob, not Esau, received Isaac's blessing. After he received his father's blessing, Jacob had to leave town because his brother Esau wanted to kill him (see Genesis 27:41-43). As he traveled toward the distant city of Haran, I'm sure Jacob thought long and hard about the events, which preceded Isaac's blessing.

Jacob's name literally means heel. He was so named because his hand grasped Esau's heel at birth (see Genesis 25:26). Jacob figuratively means, "he deceives." Unfortunately, Jacob lived up to his name. He was a deceiver. Jacob deceived his father, Isaac, and stole his brother's blessing. Esau was so angered by the deception that he wanted to murder Jacob. This left Jacob no choice but to get out of town…and fast.

It is clear that up to this point, Jacob had not lived by faith. Remember, true faith doesn't have to scheme to accomplish God's will. God had made it clear that Jacob would be heir to the promise (see Genesis 25:23). Yet Jacob and Rebekah felt they needed to manipulate circumstances so that Jacob could receive Isaac's blessing. Jacob was definitely a man who wanted to control his own life, and he was forced to suffer the consequences of his actions.

Jacob Encountered God At Bethel

At this point in the story, Jacob was tired and away from the security of home. God used the fact that Jacob was on the run to get him just where He wanted him. God is able to work all things together for good (see Romans 8:28). He planned to use Jacob's current circumstances to reveal Himself.

While he was traveling, Jacob had a dream. He saw a stairway, which reached from earth to heaven, and angels were ascending and descending on it. God was at the top of the stairway. God personally spoke to Jacob and confirmed the promises He had made to Abraham. God told Jacob that the promise would continue through his offspring. He also promised to watch over Jacob wherever he went. God promised not to leave Jacob until He fulfilled His promise.

When Jacob woke up, he thought,

> Surely the LORD is in this place, and I wasn't even aware of it…What an awesome place this is! It is none other than the house of God—the gateway to heaven! (Genesis 28:16-17 NLT)

Jacob set up a memorial pillar where this occurred, and named the place Bethel, which means "the house of God." As a result of his revelation, Jacob vowed that the Lord was his God, and the memorial pillar was God's house.

Jacob Learned To Live By Faith

Jacob had a powerful encounter with God that night at Bethel. He realized he was in the very presence of God. He saw an open heaven. The staircase provided him access. Jacob realized he had access to God, the King of all creation. Jacob discovered that there is a connection between the physical and the spiritual, between the seen and the unseen, between the visible and the invisible. Faith is that connection.

Jacob discovered how to live by faith that night. Previously, he had put his faith in himself, and made a mess of it in the process. Jacob made a commitment and turned his life over to

God. Jacob learned to focus on the unseen, rather than on what he could see with his physical eyes, because what is seen is temporary, but what is unseen is eternal (see 2 Corinthians 4:18).

Jacob Worshiped At The House Of God

Jacob's immediate reaction to his experience with God was worship. Jacob made a pillar, and named the place where he received his revelation Bethel—the house of God. Jacob declared the house of God to be a place where people would worship God, and bring Him a tithe.

In 1 Timothy 3:15, the church is called the house of God, and is described as the pillar and foundation of the truth. The church is the pillar, which God uses to reveal himself to the world today. The church is central to His plan to establish His kingdom on earth.

The local church is the house of God—the gateway to heaven. It is a place where you can encounter God. When an unbeliever visits our worship service and is saved, Green Valley becomes the place where they realized, "God was here all along and I never even knew it." For the believer, it is the place where they say, "This house of God is awesome! It is truly the gateway to encounter God!"

Jacob Blessed His Children And Grandchildren With God's Direction

At the end of his long life, Jacob gathered his sons to bless them. Jacob had twelve sons: Reuben, Simeon, Levi, Judah, Zebulun, Issachar, Dan, Gad, Asher, Naphtali, Joseph, and Benjamin.

Jacob gave a separate blessing to Joseph's two sons, Ephraim and Manasseh. He blessed both boys, but declared that

God's promise would come through Ephraim (see Genesis 48:13-20). Just like Jacob, Ephraim was the younger brother. But Jacob did not argue with God or try to change the order of the blessing, as he had years before.

Jacob learned to live by faith after his encounter with God at Bethel. When he was dying, he still realized the importance of faith, and its connection to the spiritual realm. Jacob did not hand out blessings based on what he wanted. Through worship, Jacob allowed God to direct him, and he gave the blessings according to God's will (see Hebrews 11:21).

Jacob learned that worship is the natural response to an encounter with God. To understand worship, you must have a personal encounter with God. When is the last time you personally encountered God? Perhaps it has been too long.

Don't be content to merely "go through the motions" of worship. My prayer is that you have a personal encounter with the living God and learn to live by faith. When you do, you will be able to say as Jacob did, "God is awesome in this place! He was here all along and I didn't even know it. This place is the house of God, the gate of heaven!"

Strengthen Your Faith

What are some different ways to encounter God?

Why must you encounter God before you can understand worship?

Make a commitment to experience a time of true worship this week.

22

WHEN GOOD COMES FROM BAD

By faith Joseph, when his end was near, spoke about the exodus of the Israelites from Egypt and gave instructions about his bones.
(Hebrews 11:22)

I think it was John Maxwell who said, "What happens to you is not nearly as important as what happens in you." These words are so true, especially as you contemplate your response to the difficult circumstances of life. You will inevitably experience trouble, betrayal, and tragedy. So the question is not whether you will face trouble, but how you will respond when it comes.

You cannot always control what happens to you, but you can control what happens in you. When difficulties come, you have a choice to make: you can be the victim or the victor. When you respond by faith, believing that God is in control, you will live a victorious Christian life. With God's help, you can rise above the bad circumstances that come into your life.

Joseph's Life Story

Joseph is a great example of a man who lived by faith. His story is found from Genesis 37 through Genesis 50. Joseph was Jacob's eleventh son, but was his obvious favorite because he was the firstborn of Jacob's beloved wife Rachel. He may have been his father's favorite, but Joseph's brothers hated him. Joseph was known as a dreamer and on two separate occasions, dreamt he would one-day rule over his brothers. When he shared these dreams with his brothers, they hated him all the more.

One day, his brothers decided to kill him. Reuben convinced the brothers not to kill Joseph, so they sold him into slavery. They hid their crime from their father by claiming Joseph was killed by a wild animal. Ishmaelite slave traders took Joseph to Egypt and sold him to a man named Potiphar, who was one of the pharaoh's officials.

Joseph worked hard and was promoted to the highest position in Potiphar's household. Potiphar's wife wanted to have an affair with Joseph. When he refused, she accused him of attempted rape and Joseph was thrown in prison.

God was with Joseph in prison, and so the warden looked favorably upon him. He was placed over all of the prisoners. While in prison, Joseph met the pharaoh's baker and cupbearer and interpreted their dreams. He asked the cupbearer to remember him when he was released from prison, but the cupbearer did not.

Two years later, the pharaoh had a dream that no one could interpret. At that point, the cupbearer told the pharaoh about Joseph. Joseph explained the pharaoh's dream, predicting seven years of abundance, followed by seven years of famine. Because the spirit of God gave him discernment, Joseph was appointed to be in charge of the food storage program, which was implemented to prepare for the famine. When the famine hit, Joseph was second in command in all of Egypt.

Joseph married Asenath and had two sons. He named his firstborn Manasseh, "because God has made me forget all my trouble and all my father's household" (Genesis 41:51). His second son was named Ephraim, "because God has made me fruitful in the land of my suffering" (Genesis 41:52).

Because the famine extended to Canaan, Joseph's brothers eventually came to Egypt to buy grain. Joseph recognized them but did not reveal his true identity. Instead, he accused them of being spies and held Simeon prisoner until they brought his younger brother, Benjamin, to Egypt. This was a test to see if they had changed over the years. When Jacob was told what happened, he refused to send Benjamin. However, Jacob was forced to change his mind due to the continued food shortage.

When Benjamin appeared before Joseph, Joseph wept. Joseph returned Simeon to his family and sent them on their way. However, they were stopped en route and Benjamin was accused of stealing Joseph's silver cup. The brothers returned to face Joseph. Joseph said Benjamin had to stay in Egypt as his slave. Judah begged Joseph to take him in Benjamin's place.

Joseph revealed himself to his brothers. The brothers feared Joseph would exact revenge, but Joseph genuinely forgave his brothers. Judah's intervention on Benjamin's behalf showed Joseph that his brothers had changed. He invited Jacob and his brothers to live in Egypt. They settled in Goshen.

Joseph saw the misfortune he encountered in life from a faith perspective. Joseph said, "You intended to harm me, but God intended it for good to accomplish what is now being done, the saving of many lives" (Genesis 50:20).

Joseph lived 110 years. Before his death, he said,

> "I am about to die. But God will surely come to your aid and take you up out of this land to the land he promised on oath to Abraham, Isaac and Jacob." And Joseph made the sons of Israel swear an oath and said, "God will surely come to your aid, and then you must carry my bones up from this place." (Genesis 50:24-25)

Joseph Exhibited Faith In All Circumstances

If anyone knew about trouble, it was Joseph. Think back to what happened to him. He was raised in a very dysfunctional family. Jealousy consumed his brothers to the point of hatred. They planned to kill Joseph, but opted instead to sell him into slavery. Talk about the ultimate family betrayal! He was forced to work as a slave. While he was innocently going about his duties, he was tempted with adultery, and ran away. Joseph did the right thing because he knew adultery was a sin against God. However, he was falsely accused of rape and thrown into prison. In other words, he was punished for doing the right thing. And finally, those Joseph helped during his wrongful incarceration forgot about him.

Yes, Joseph had it bad, but his faith sustained him. Every time life dealt Joseph a bad blow, he got back up. He did not feel sorry for himself, and he never gave up. Joseph did more than survive; he rose to the top, again and again, because the Lord was with him. Everyone who knew Joseph realized that God was with him. Joseph relied on God in each situation, and moved forward, by faith.

Joseph saw that his personal suffering was for a greater good. It enabled his family to survive during the famine, so that God's promise would be fulfilled through his descendants. Joseph said,

> But God sent me ahead of you to preserve for you a remnant on earth and to save your lives by a great deliverance. So then, it was not you who sent me here, but God. (Genesis 45:7-8)

Faith For Your Circumstances

Joseph experienced hard times. Maybe you can relate to some of his experiences. Were you raised in a dysfunctional family, or is your own family currently messed up? Do you know how it feels to be the object of someone's extreme jealousy or hatred? Have you experienced a family betrayal, or sexual temptation? Were you ever penalized for doing the right thing? Has a person you previously helped forgotten you in your hour of need?

It us unlikely you have been the victim of an intended murder plot, sold into slavery, or been wrongfully imprisoned. But your tragic circumstances may include situations which Joseph never encountered, such as: alcohol or drug addiction, molestation, an unplanned pregnancy, the inability to go to college, a job lay-off, emotional depression, an incurable disease, or financial difficulties. Unfortunately, the list of negative circumstances in which you might find yourself is endless.

The victim mentality has taken over in many areas of society. It is not uncommon to hear someone say, "It is not my fault. I am this way because…," or, "I cannot do this because.…" You fill in the blank. Someone who makes a statement like that shows they have little or no faith. Faith believes that with God, all things are possible.

There is beauty in the way Joseph named his two sons. He named his firstborn Manasseh, which means God helped me forget the evil done to me in the past. This does not imply that Joseph had no recollection of what happened to him. His past experiences were very real, and should not be discounted. It means that God took the anger and bitterness out of his past experiences. Joseph moved on, with God's help. Past events had no control over him, because Joseph chose to be controlled by the spirit of God.

God delivered Joseph, and He can do the same for you. God can help you leave your past where it belongs…in the past. By faith, allow God to free you from replaying past experiences over and over again in your mind. Put aside the anger and bitterness, which poison you. Put your life in His hands, and watch your faith increase.

Joseph named his second son Ephraim, which means, God made me fruitful in the land of my suffering. God allowed Joseph to struggle. But Joseph's faith was strengthened by what happened to him. God used Joseph mightily. He was fruitful despite his circumstances. Joseph, a hero of faith, did not allow his circumstances to derail him from his God-intended purpose.

God can use any circumstance for good, even if it was meant for evil. Let the story of Joseph show you that your circumstances are not as important as how you respond. The choice is yours, you can live as a victim, and allow your past to adversely affect your future, or you can come to the point where you trust God with your circumstances, and rise above them.

Strengthen Your Faith

Respond to the statement, "What happens to you is not nearly as important as what happens in you."

Read Genesis 45:7-8. Explain how Joseph exhibited faith in all circumstances.

How do you respond when faced with difficult circumstances?

Meditate on Romans 8:28 today.

23

MAKING DECISIONS BY FAITH

> *By faith Moses' parents hid him for three months after he was born, because they saw he was no ordinary child, and they were not afraid of the king's edict.*
> (Hebrews 11:23)

Making decisions is an everyday part of life. Some decisions are easy and others are more difficult. On a daily basis, you must decide what you will wear, what you will eat, and what you will do. There are also times when you must make life-changing decisions, such as where you will go to college, whom you will marry, and how you will respond to Jesus Christ. Yes, life is filled with decisions, and it sometimes takes great courage to make a decision by faith.

I love the story of Eric Liddell in the movie *Chariots of Fire*. Liddell was Britain's greatest hope for a gold medal in the 1924 summer Olympics. Known as "The Flying Scotsman," his event was the 100-meter dash. When he arrived at the Olympics, Liddell learned that his race would be run on a Sunday. Being a devout Christian, he felt he shouldn't compete on Sunday.

Eric Liddell prayed earnestly and made a decision by faith. He chose not to run on Sunday. Eric stood true to his convictions, even though he knew the consequences would be severe. After he announced his decision not to run, Britain came back with a new proposal. They offered him a spot in the 400-meter race, which was not run on Sunday. Although it was not his best event, Liddell agreed. He competed in the 400 and won the gold medal.

Just like Eric Liddell, you will be faced with some important decisions in your lifetime. Most significant decisions involve some type of risk and may require you to take a step of faith. Sometimes they even make the difference between life and death, as was the case in today's Scripture. Moses' parents were forced to make a decision: they chose to defy the law in order to protect their son.

The Story Of Moses' Birth

God told Abraham that his descendants would be strangers in a country not their own, and they would be enslaved and mistreated for four hundred years. As the four hundred years was nearing an end, God put into motion His plan to set His people free from slavery.

The pharaoh of Egypt felt threatened by the population explosion among the Hebrews. He ordered that every male Hebrew baby born must be thrown into the Nile River. Moses was born during this time. His mother's name was Jochebed, and his father was Amram.

By faith Moses' parents decided they would not allow their child to be thrown into the Nile. They were aware of the potential consequences of this decision, but believed by faith that this was what God wanted them to do. So they disobeyed the pharaoh's law, which required Moses be killed, and hid him for three months.

When they could no longer hide him, they made a papyrus basket, and coated it with tar. They laid Moses in the basket and placed it in the reeds of the Nile River. Moses' sister Miriam stayed in the area to see what would happen. Pharaoh's daughter found the basket as she was bathing. She knew the baby was a Hebrew and felt sorry for him, and took him as her own. Miriam approached the pharaoh's daughter, and asked her if she needed someone to nurse the baby. When she said yes, Miriam brought her mother to the princess. Pharaoh's daughter paid Jochebed to nurse Moses.

When Moses grew older, he went to live with the pharaoh's daughter and became her son. "Moses was educated in all the wisdom of the Egyptians and was powerful in speech and action" (Acts 7:22). Pharaoh's daughter named Moses. His name means, "I drew him out of the water."

Moses' Parents And Sister Made Decisions By Faith

Moses' parents are listed in the faith hall of fame. By faith, they realized that Moses was no ordinary child. They knew God had something important planned for Moses, and so they made the decision to hide their son. They were not afraid of the king's edict. They refused to kill their child, but there was nothing they could do to change the law. Their decision to disobey the law was made by faith.

When they could no longer hide Moses, they placed him in a basket in the Nile River. This was another decision of faith, because they did know what would happen to Moses once he was found. They trusted God to protect their son, and He did. The pharaoh's daughter found Moses and decided to adopt him.

By faith, Miriam made the decision to go and speak with the pharaoh's daughter about the baby. She arranged for her own mother to nurse and care for Moses. Miriam took a tremendous risk when she introduced the pharaoh's daughter to the family of the child she had found. It was a risk, which required faith.

God honored the faith of Moses' parents and sister. He allowed Moses to live with his Hebrew family during his early, formative years. During that time, his parents taught him about

God, and the promises He had made. Moses was able to learn the foundations of his faith from his own family. His parents made the most of the opportunity to pass down their faith. When Moses grew older, he went to live at the palace. There he was educated in the wisdom of the Egyptians, which was all part of God's plan.

Courageous Faith

Courage is possible at all times, because God is with you. He will never leave you nor forsake you. That is a promise. If you are a Christian, you are indwelled by the Holy Spirit. He lives within you and will always be with you (see John 14:17). Because Jesus lives in you, you can be courageous. He is greater than anything or anyone in the world (see 1 John 4:4).

God wants you to have a faith that overcomes fear. He wants you to be courageous, and stand firm in your faith. 1 Corinthians 16:13 says, "Be on your guard; stand firm in the faith; be men of courage; be strong." Do not lose confidence in God. He does not want you to shrink back from your faith. God calls it shrinking back when you do not trust Him. It is a sign of weak faith. God wants you to live by faith, so if you shrink back from doing His will, He is not pleased (see Hebrews 10:38). Remember, without faith, it is impossible to please God (see Hebrews 11:6).

The parents of Moses did not allow their circumstances to paralyze them with fear. They focused their eyes of faith on God and trusted Him to provide a way out. Because they lived by faith, they were able to make the right decisions. Fear cannot stop strong faith. God wants you to develop courageous faith. When you act with courage, you show that your faith is real.

Strengthen Your Faith

Describe a time in your life when you had to make a difficult decision.

What role does courage play in the journey of faith?

How does living by faith enable you to make right decisions?

24

HUMILITY

By faith Moses, when he had grown up, refused to be known as the son of Pharaoh's daughter.
(Hebrews 11:24)

It was the worst day of my life! Sometimes it takes a horrible experience before you learn to depend on God. As a recent college graduate, I had a good job, a nice apartment, a new car, and a pretty girlfriend. I was on my way to realizing all of my dreams...until the infamous day when my girlfriend of two years dumped me for another guy. This unexpected change in plans left me feeling like a failure. I was embarrassed, humiliated, and didn't know what to do.

God finally had my attention. For the first time in my life, I started depending on God instead of Rob. You see, although I was a Christian, I had given God control of my life in name only. When I gave God control of the actual day-to-day operations, He revealed a different plan for my future. God's plan required that I leave my job, my security; the life I had known, to follow Him completely. At first it was scary. I did not understand. But the more I learned to trust God and give Him control of my life, the easier it became.

Through a series of events, including a mission trip and a week at a rehab center with my alcoholic father, God revealed His plan for my life. I suddenly realized that my life was not going to be about a good job, a nice apartment, a new car, or even a girlfriend. God had something better for me. To receive it, I had to leave all the other "stuff" behind.

I resigned from my job, and canceled my lease, leaving behind all I had known to follow God. I enrolled in seminary and moved to New Orleans. The hardest part was the humiliation of downsizing, selling off many of my possessions, and moving to a new city without any income. Some of my coworkers considered me a quitter; others just didn't understand. Friends and family thought I had lost my marbles! But there was no doubt in my mind what God wanted me to do.

It took hitting rock bottom, after the breakup of an important relationship, for me to look up to God. That embarrassing and humiliating experience was a turning point in my life. At the time, it seemed as if I was the only one in the world who had experienced such humiliation, but I later learned I was in good company.

Moses Flees To Midian

Consider Moses. He was the envy of all young men. As a prince of Egypt, Moses lived in a palace, wore the nicest clothes, and always had plenty of money. But Moses' circumstances changed in the blink of an eye. One day, as Moses was overseeing a work crew, he saw an Egyptian man beat a Hebrew slave. Moses realized the Egyptian man was hurting his own people. When he thought no one was looking, Moses killed the Egyptian and hid him in the sand. By killing the Egyptian, Moses thought his own people would realize that God was using him to rescue them, but they did not.

The next day Moses went out and saw two Israelites fighting and tried to reconcile them. He asked the men why they were fighting among their own people. One answered, "Who made you our judge and ruler? Are you going to kill us just like you killed the Egyptian?" Moses became frightened his murder had become common knowledge. When the pharaoh heard what Moses did, he tried to kill him.

Moses fled to Midian. Moses married his wife, Zipporah, while in Midian. He also had a son. He named his son, Gershom, which means, "I have become an alien in a foreign land" (Exodus 2:22). The king of Egypt died and the Israelites groaned under their yoke of slavery. God heard their cry and was concerned.

After forty years as a shepherd, Moses received a dramatic call to the ministry. The angel of the Lord appeared to Moses in a burning bush (it was on fire but did not burn up). God called out to Moses and told him to take off his sandals, because he was standing on holy ground. God told Moses that He planned to rescue the Israelites. Moses was to bring the people out of Egypt and take them to the Promised Land. Moses responded, "Who am I, that I should go to Pharaoh and bring the Israelites out of Egypt?" (Exodus 3:11).

God promised to be with Moses. Moses was to tell the Israelites I AM WHO I AM sent him. God would enable Moses to perform miraculous signs for the elders as proof that God sent him. God showed Moses the signs in advance to help calm Moses' fears. God said Moses was to be His representative, but Aaron could be the spokesman.

Moses Gives Up His Privileged Position

Moses lived the first forty years of his life as a prince in Egypt. Egypt was the most advanced society of its time. Moses was highly educated and skilled and was part of the royal court. The whole world was open to him.

But Moses never forgot the training he received from his birth parents. They instilled in him, at a very young age, a deep love for God. They taught Moses about God's promises. Moses never forgot the foundations of faith that his parents taught him before he moved to the palace.

The training he received in the palace was not able to weaken his faith. He believed God and His promises. At the age of forty, Moses came to a fork in the road. He had to decide whether he would live his life as an Egyptian, or a Hebrew. By faith, Moses chose to stand with his people. He refused to be known as the son of Pharaoh's daughter (see Hebrews 11:24). Moses' mission was to protect God's people by defying the pharaoh.

By faith, Moses knew that God had chosen him for a special purpose. Moses knew he was to rescue his people, and that is why he killed the Egyptian. Moses thought, when he avenged his fellow Israelite, his people would realize God was using him to rescue them. They did not. The pharaoh wanted Moses dead for killing the Egyptian, and Moses was forced to flee to Midian. It was still not God's appointed time to deliver the Israelites.

It was never God's intention for Moses to murder the Egyptian, but God used this circumstance to begin a new type of training. Moses spent the next forty years as a shepherd in Midian. Moses needed to learn some very practical and important skills, which were not part of his extensive Egyptian education. Moses learned to find his way around the desert and wilderness area of Sinai. This taught him basic survival skills, and patience. As a shepherd, Moses also honed his leadership skills. This was all part of God's plan to prepare Moses to lead the Israelites out of Egypt into the very wilderness where he had lived for forty years.

God Teaches Moses Humility

God wanted to use Moses for a tremendous purpose, but Moses needed to learn humility first. When he was forty years old, Moses tried to liberate the Israelites on his own. Moses' plan was to free his people, and invite God along for the ride. When he acted apart from God, Moses found himself in serious trouble. He was forced to run for his life.

Moses needed to learn humility, and he spent forty years in the desert doing just that. Moses learned his lesson well. Numbers 12:3 describes Moses as "a very humble man, more humble than anyone else on the face of the earth." After spending forty years as a shepherd, Moses demonstrated how he had changed. He humbly responded to God's call by saying, "Who am I that I should be called to do this?"

The Importance Of Humility

God values the humble (see Isaiah 66:2). He hates pride (see Proverbs 8:13). God transformed Moses, who started out as a proud member of the Egyptian royal family, into a humble man. God is willing to do whatever it takes to teach you humility as well.

What I thought was a horrible circumstance in my life, God used for my ultimate good. I was humbled and learned to depend totally on Him. The same is true for you. God can use a bad circumstance in your life to humble you, so that you learn to depend on Him. When you humble yourself before God, you prove that you value Him above all else, including self. It is then that God can do a great work in your life and use you to accomplish great things for His kingdom.

Strengthen Your Faith

Describe a time when you hit rock bottom and it caused you to look up to God.

What lessons do you think Moses learned during his forty years in the desert?

What situations has God used to teach you humility?

Do something that requires humility today. Pray for a humble heart.

25

CHOOSING TO LIVE FOR GOD

He [Moses] chose to be mistreated along with the people of God rather than to enjoy the pleasures of sin for a short time.
(Hebrews 11:25)

John D. Rockefeller was a man who had it all. At an early age he determined he wanted to make a lot of money. He was a millionaire by the age of thirty-three and by age fifty-three was the richest man in the world. No one had it better than John D. Rockefeller.

But something happened soon after, which would change his life forever. Rockefeller developed a severe case of alopecia, which caused his body to deteriorate. He had all the money in the world but his daily diet consisted of milk and crackers. In addition, Rockefeller's pursuit of money and power had created many enemies. He was forced to hire a personal bodyguard for protection. The quality of his life declined to the point that he could no longer enjoy the pleasures of the world.

Rockefeller's doctors believed he had less than a year to live. During this time, something happened, which the doctors were unable to explain. In the privacy of his bedroom, Rockefeller called out to God. When he awoke the next morning, his entire countenance had changed. He was a new man. Rockefeller began using his wealth to help others. He gave money to churches and charities. He also established the

Rockefeller Foundation, which is still an active philanthropic organization.

Although doctors had predicted he would live less than a year, John D. Rockefeller lived forty-five more years and died at the age of ninety-eight. Friends and family said he was completely transformed, when he made the choice to stop living for self.

You, too, must make a choice. You can choose to live for self or you can choose to live for God. I love what the Bible says in Joshua 24:15.

> But if serving the LORD seems undesirable to you, then choose for yourselves this day whom you will serve, whether the gods your forefathers served beyond the River, or the gods of the Amorites, in whose land you are living. But as for me and my household, we will serve the LORD.

By Faith Moses Chose To Live For God

Hebrews 11:25 deals with the issue of lifestyle. As a Christian, you have the choice to follow God by faith, or to live for the world. This is an important decision that hits at the very heart of how you choose to live. If you choose to enjoy the pleasures of sin, you are a worldly Christian. In other words, the things of the world are of greater value to you than the things of God. This results in broken fellowship with God. The phrase "the pleasures of sin" does not merely refer to sexual sins. It refers to a lifestyle of sin, whereby a believer lives life independent of God.

Moses had a very strong faith, which was demonstrated by the difficult decision he made. He gave up his wealth, status, and power to stand with God. Moses could not enjoy his luxurious lifestyle, while the Israelites lived in agony.

In the eyes of the world, Moses gave up everything. He became nothing more than a lowly shepherd. But Moses knew he had lost nothing. Moses viewed life through eyes of faith and understood that God's is the only opinion that matters. I believe it was missionary Jim Elliot who said, "He is no fool who gives what he cannot keep to gain what he cannot lose."

A Believer Is A New Creation In Christ

When you are saved, your old, sinful nature is crucified and dies. Your old self is gone. You become a new creation (see 2 Corinthians 5:17). Your new nature is placed into your existing body. In other words, you are a brand-new person on the inside, but your exterior has not changed.

The Difference Between A Carnal Christian And A Spirit-Filled Christian

As a believer, you will experience a constant battle between your physical body, and your new nature. Your body desperately wants you to maintain your old habits, which are the result of your sinful nature. The *Holy* Spirit, inside of you, does not want you to continue sinning (see 1 John 3:9). So a battle rages on inside of you. You must choose who wins.

If your lifestyle is difficult to distinguish from the rest of the world, you are a carnal Christian. Tony Evans defines a carnal Christian as a believer who "knowingly, intentionally, and persistently lives to please and serve self rather than God."[1] In other words, they adopt a "sinful pattern of life."[2]

A carnal Christian does whatever they want, regardless of what the Bible says on the subject. Their most important goal is to please themselves and reach their own objectives: wealth, power, prestige, popularity, recognition, the right connections, and an easy lifestyle. They do not care about what God wants. Some Christians are very blatant in their trek toward success. Other believers mask their carnality with the trappings of religion. Either way, a carnal Christian values the world and self more highly than God.

If you are saved, you should no longer live for yourself, but for Jesus. To live for Jesus, you must choose to put off your old self and its sinful desires (see Ephesians 4:22). You must take off your old self and put to death whatever belongs to your earthly nature. Do whatever is necessary to rid yourself of these sins (see Colossians 3:5-9).

If you want to be a Spirit-filled Christian, you must put on your new self (see Colossians 3:10), which is created to be like God (see Ephesians 4:24). But, how do you do this? Proverbs 23:7 in the Amplified Bible says, *"For as he thinks* in his heart, *so is he"* (emphasis added). The Boyd paraphrase: "You are what you think."

The transformation process starts in your mind (see Ephesians 4:23). You must learn to set your mind on what the Holy Spirit desires (see Romans 8:5), because whatever controls your mind controls your actions. Galatians 5:25 in the Amplified Bible teaches that when you live by the Spirit, the Spirit controls your conduct. When you fill your mind with what the Spirit desires, the Spirit controls how you walk, talk and behave. This is the key to the Spirit-filled life.

<u>You Must Choose How You Will Live</u>

Moses had to decide whether he would live God's way, or follow the ways of the world. This is a choice that you must make as well. And, unfortunately, it is not a one-time decision. It is an issue that will continually surface throughout your journey of faith.

If you are not currently living your life for God, you can change. You do not have to conform to this world. You can be transformed by the renewing of your mind (see Romans 12:2).

I would like to close with The Message paraphrase of Romans 12:1-2.

> So here's what I want you to do, God helping you: Take your everyday, ordinary life—your sleeping, eating, going-to-work, and walking-around life—and place it before God as an offering. Embracing what God does for you is the best thing you can do for him. *Don't become so well-adjusted to your culture that you fit into it without even thinking. Instead, fix your attention on God. You'll be changed from the inside out.* Readily recognize what he wants from you, and quickly respond to it. Unlike the culture around you, always dragging you down to its level of immaturity, God brings the best out of you, develops well-formed maturity in you (emphasis added).

Strengthen Your Faith

Describe what it means to be a worldly Christian.

Read Romans 7:15. Describe how this verse relates to your life.

How can you "choose" to be a Spirit-filled Christian?

Make a list of the sins that pull you down. Confess them to God and choose today to live the Spirit-filled life.

26

WHEN PERSECUTION COMES

*He [Moses] regarded disgrace for the sake of
Christ as of greater value than the treasures of
Egypt, because he was looking ahead
to his reward.*
(Hebrews 11:26)

    Braveheart, starring Mel Gibson, is a movie based on the life of William Wallace. As a young Scottish boy, William Wallace saw his family brutally murdered by officers of the English army. He went to live with an uncle in a distant land, and there grew in knowledge and strength. When Wallace returned to Scotland, he secretly married his childhood sweetheart. It was necessary to conceal the marriage in order to protect his wife from a horrific English law, requiring every Scottish bride to spend her wedding night with an English officer. When word of Wallace's marriage reached the English, they came for his wife. She refused to comply with the immoral law, and was brutally murdered in the center of the village.
    This despicable act set a fire deep within the soul of William Wallace. He became the leader of a resistance movement, which sought to free Scotland from English rule in the thirteenth century. In the years following his wife's death, Wallace passionately led the people to stand up for freedom. However, he was ultimately betrayed by one of his own countrymen and handed over to England for a public execution.

On the day of his execution, Wallace was told that if he pled for mercy his death would be swift. He refused. Wallace considered suffering for the cause of freedom to be of greater value than his own life. Each time the executioner gave him a chance to beg for mercy, he refused. This caused the torture to escalate. The crowd became distraught by the appalling scene and begged Wallace to cry "mercy."

Finally, when it seemed as if his body could take no more, Wallace indicated a desire to speak. The officers came close and the crowd quickly became silent. With everything he had, William Wallace yelled, "FREEDOM!...FREEDOM!...FREEDOM!" With that one word, his earthly life came to an end.

Moses Was Willing To Suffer For The Messiah

Take a moment and read today's Scripture in two other translations:

> He valued suffering in the Messiah's camp far greater than Egyptian wealth because he was looking ahead, anticipating the payoff. (Hebrews 11:26 MSG)

> He thought it was better to suffer for the sake of the Messiah than to own the treasures of Egypt, for he was looking ahead to the great reward that God would give him. (Hebrews 11:26 NLT)

Moses looked away from the wealth of the world. He considered suffering and persecution *with* God preferable to all the treasures of Egypt *apart* from God. Moses felt Christ was worth being disgraced in the eyes of the world. He felt any suffering was worth it to gain Christ.

You Will Suffer For The Sake Of Christ

There are many verses in the New Testament, which indicate Christ is worth disgrace and suffering. For example:

> If you are insulted because of the name of Christ, you are blessed, for the Spirit of glory and of God rests on you. (1 Peter 4:14)

> However, if you suffer as a Christian, do not be ashamed, but praise God that you bear that name. (1 Peter 4:16)

> I consider that our present sufferings are not worth comparing with the glory that will be revealed in us. (Romans 8:18)

> Blessed are those who are persecuted because of righteousness, for theirs is the kingdom of heaven. Blessed are you *when* people insult you, persecute you and falsely say all kinds of evil against you because of me. Rejoice and be glad, because great is your reward in heaven, for in the same way they persecuted the prophets who were before you. (Matthew 5:10-12, emphasis added)

God considers persecution for the sake of Christ a blessing, which should cause you to rejoice. The very fact that you are persecuted is proof of your faithfulness. People will only insult you, laugh at you, and talk bad about you if your faith is obvious to those around you. If your faith is weak, no one will even notice your relationship to Christ. It would be a waste of time to persecute you on Jesus' behalf.

Matthew 5:11 uses the word "when," rather than "if" in reference to persecution. That indicates persecution is inevitable if you live your life committed to Christ. Do not be surprised when you are persecuted. Men will hate you because of Christ (see Luke 21:17). This opposition will not come only from nonbelievers. Persecution often comes from carnal Christians who feel you threaten their status quo or traditions. Persecution and suffering might even come from your spouse, family or close friends (e.g. Judas).

You Will Be Rewarded For Persecution

If you are disgraced or experience suffering in this world on behalf of Jesus, great is your reward in heaven. Your future reward is far better than anything you could receive in this life. Rejoice because there is a direct correlation between what you do on earth and your reward, or inheritance, in heaven.

Strong Faith Is Willing To Suffer Disgrace For Christ

Moses knew that disgrace and suffering for Christ was of greater value than all the wealth and treasures of Egypt. He gladly gave up everything the world had to offer. He chose to live for God, and never returned to his old way of life.

In the same way, you are to live completely for Jesus and His kingdom. What you gain in Jesus is better than anything this world has to offer. But do not be surprised when you are persecuted for your faith. Persecution proves the world has noticed your stand for Christ.

Endure your suffering in the same way Jesus did. "When they hurled insults at him, he did not retaliate; when he suffered, he made no threats. Instead, he entrusted himself to him who judges justly" (1 Peter 2:23). By faith, face persecution and suffering, knowing that God is in control. When you suffer for Christ's sake, God sees your faith and is very pleased.

How you respond to the suffering and persecution you experience on behalf of Christ is completely up to you. William Wallace thought it was more important to stand for freedom than to reduce his pain. His example motivated the Scottish people to secure their independence from England. An entire nation was moved by the courage of one man.

In Acts 5:41 the Bible says, "The apostles left the Sanhedrin, rejoicing because they had been counted worthy of suffering disgrace for the Name." The disciples rejoiced because God considered them worthy of persecution for the cause of Christ. They counted it an honor to suffer for the name of Jesus.

Because you live in America, you have experienced relatively little persecution for the sake of Christ. However, that is not true in other parts of the world. In Indonesia and Pakistan, Christians can lose their homes, families, even their lives if they believe in Jesus. How do they respond? They rejoice.

What about you? How will you respond when persecution comes? I pray you will lean on the faith of Moses, the disciples, and every believer who has gone before you. Most of all, remember the words of Jesus when He said, "Rejoice and be glad, because great is your reward in heaven!" (Matthew 5:12).

Strengthen Your Faith

Describe a time in your life when you suffered, or were persecuted, for your faith.

How does your suffering or persecution compare to what is endured by Christians in other countries?

What are you willing to die for?

Meditate on the words of Jesus in Matthew 5:10-12.

27

THE FEAR OF GOD

By faith he left Egypt, not fearing the king's anger; he persevered because he saw him who is invisible.
(Hebrews 11:27)

When I was in seminary, people knew which professors were easy and which ones were hard. I was told to avoid Dr. Harrison for Old Testament if I was concerned about my grade point average. He was considered the toughest professor on campus. The older students said he regularly failed 60% of his class.

Most of the students at my seminary didn't like Dr. Harrison. As for me, I loved his class and his teaching methods. When I began seminary, I was an accountant and had much to learn about the Bible. Grades were not my primary concern. I was there to learn as much as I could. There was no doubt that Dr. Harrison knew the Old Testament better than anyone, so I signed up for his class. I sat under him four days a week and absorbed his every word.

For many years I kept a file in my office, which was a reminder of my first Old Testament class. In that file was my first Old Testament exam, which every person in the class failed. I received a grade of 39%! (I don't think even Moses could have passed that test!) Most students dropped the class when they saw their test score. Others protested to the president. I sat on the front row, listened and learned. By the end of the semester, I had a B. I took two more classes under him and made A's.

I never questioned Dr. Harrison's teaching methods. I feared him too much for that. I was in awe of who he was and respected what he wished to accomplish in my life. I knew Dr. Harrison had my best interest at heart. On the first day of class, Dr. Harrison said that if I sat under his teaching and followed his instructions, I would learn the Old Testament in a way I would never forget. Today, I attribute my ability to tell biblical stories to Dr. Harrison. He brought the Old Testament to life. Every time I tell an Old Testament story, I remember the days when I sat in fear on the front row of his class.

Today's Scripture says that Moses did not fear the king of Egypt. His fear of an earthly king was superseded by his fear of God. The fear of God is a profound respect and reverence for who God is and what He can do. So great was Moses' respect for God, that the pharaoh paled in comparison. Remember, Moses had encountered God up close and personal. Out of the burning bush he was told to take off his sandals because he was standing on holy ground. Without even thinking, out of fear and reverence to the Lord, Moses obeyed and fell to the ground.

Moses Delivers The Israelites From Slavery

God instructed Moses to return to Egypt and lead the Israelites out of slavery. When he arrived, Moses told Pharaoh to let the Israelites hold a festival to God in the desert. Pharaoh said he did not know the Lord and refused Moses' request. To spite God, Pharaoh increased the oppression on the slaves. This caused the people to grumble against Moses.

Moses warned Pharaoh that God would perform miraculous signs and wonders in Egypt, and would judge Egypt for failing to let the Israelites go. But Pharaoh's heart was hard. God unleashed ten plagues in Egypt (see Exodus 7:14-12:30). After the tenth plague, the death of the firstborn, Pharaoh ordered Moses and the Israelites to quickly leave the country. Pharaoh later changed his mind. He did not want to lose all of his slave labor, so he began to chase the Israelites. When the Israelites saw the pharaoh closing in on them, they complained to Moses.

Moses Did Not Fear Man

Moses had good reason to be fearful. First, God wanted Moses to meet with the pharaoh of Egypt, which was a very intimidating experience. Second, Moses was a fugitive. He was on the run for killing an Egyptian slave driver when he was forty. Third, Moses had to present God's plan that Pharaoh release the slaves. His message was guaranteed to provoke the pharaoh's anger.

The first meeting did not go well. Pharaoh was dead-set against God's plan to free the Israelites. This required Moses to meet with Pharaoh repeatedly. By God's power, Moses inflicted ten plagues on the country. This made Moses the most unpopular man in Egypt!

Moses also experienced problems within his own community. When Moses first arrived in Egypt and told the Israelites of God's plan, they were all excited. They probably said something like, "Yes, Moses, you're the man! We're all behind you." But as the pressure of their situation increased, Moses' own people began to turn on him. They grumbled and complained about him (see Exodus 5:20-21; Exodus 6:9; Exodus 14:11-12). Moses did so much for those people, and all they could do was complain that they were better off without him.

Despite the pressure he was under, Moses did not fear the king's anger (see Hebrews 11:27). Moses knew his purpose was to deliver the Israelites from slavery in Egypt. It did not matter whether he experienced opposition from the Egyptians, or from his own people. His profound respect and reverence for God far outweighed the fear of his current situation. Moses knew God's will, and nothing would stop him.

Moses Used His Shield Of Faith To Block Fear

Satan knows the righteous live by faith and that without faith it is impossible to please God. He will stop at nothing in his attempt to destroy your faith. Fear is a very powerful weapon in his arsenal. Satan loves to put terror and dread into your heart. But Moses had a secret weapon against fear: his shield of faith. Faith can extinguish all the flaming arrows of the evil one (see Ephesians 6:16).

God promised Moses that he would rescue His people. God promised to be with Moses as he spoke to Pharaoh and led the Israelites out of Egypt. By faith, Moses never doubted the outcome of God's promises. He was certain of what he could not see because he knew and feared God.

Moses Feared God

What does it mean to fear God? It does not mean you live in constant fear that God will zap you when you mess up. The fear of God is awe, or reverence directed toward God. It is a profound respect for God's holiness, sovereignty, mercy, power, wisdom, grace, and love. To fear God is to know and understand who He is.

Did you know that God wants you to know Him? (see Hosea 6:6 NLT). This requires more than the assimilation of facts about God (e.g. God is powerful and eternal). To know God requires a relationship. God reveals Himself when you seek

Him with all of your heart (see Deuteronomy 4:29). The more intimate your relationship, the more you will know Him.

In the Bible, people who knew God were strong and able to carry out great exploits. Moses knew and feared God. Because of this, he was able to stand strong against the pharaoh and lead the Israelites out of Egypt.

Moses moved forward and took courageous action on behalf of God's people. But Moses' strength was balanced with humility. He was a very humble man. God had previously taught Moses the importance of humility.

Lift Your Shield Of Faith

Each day, in his journey of faith, Moses learned more about God. The more he knew God, the more he feared God. When he focused on who God is, Moses realized there was no reason to be frightened by those who opposed him.

Moses' secret weapon, a shield of faith, is available to you. People and situations need not cause you to fear. Remember, God is love (see 1 John 4:16). There is no fear in love. Perfect love drives out fear (see 1 John 4:18).

When you fear God, you need not fear anything in the world. You can develop such a respect for who God is and what He is doing, that you know He has your best interest at heart. God promises that if you sit under His teaching and follow the instructions in His Word, you have no reason to fear.

Strengthen Your Faith

Describe something you fear.

How would you define the fear of God?

Name several circumstances, which should have caused Moses to be afraid?

Meditate on 1 John 4:18.

28

POWER IN THE BLOOD

By faith he kept the Passover and the sprinkling of blood, so that the destroyer of the firstborn would not touch the firstborn of Israel.
(Hebrews 11:28)

  Joe Abrams was the Music Director in the first church where I served as Pastor. The church was small and could not afford a full-time worship leader. Joe, a seasoned college music professor, worked part time at the church. Together, we made a great team. He provided wisdom and experience, while I added vision and energy. I will always cherish the three years I served alongside Joe Abrams.
  Joe's favorite song was actually the chorus of an old hymn—"There Is Power in the Blood." The chorus of this hymn says:

> There is pow'r, pow'r,
> Wonder working pow'r,
> In the blood of the Lamb;
> There is pow'r, pow'r,
> Wonder working pow'r,
> In the precious blood of the Lamb.
>
> (Lewis E. Jones, public domain)

  Joe could make this old chorus come to life. He would

shake his fist at every mention of the word "power," and the church always responded enthusiastically. They sang with gusto. Even if some of the worshipers didn't fully comprehend the significance of the blood, it was evident to everyone in attendance that the blood of the Lamb was special. Today you will take a closer look at why the blood of the Lamb is so important.

The Passover

God told Moses that the tenth plague would kill the firstborn son of every Egyptian (including Pharaoh) and their cattle. However, God provided Moses with Passover instructions, which were to be carefully explained to all in the Hebrew community. God told Moses that any Hebrew who followed His directions would be spared from the tenth plague.

Moses gave God's Passover instructions to the people. He told each Hebrew family to slaughter a perfect lamb, and place some of the lamb's blood on the sides and top of their doorframe (see Exodus 12:5-7). The blood on the doorframe would serve as a sign that the plague should pass over, or skip that household. God said,

> On that same night I will pass through Egypt and strike down every firstborn—both men and animals—and I will bring judgment on all the gods of Egypt. I am the LORD. The blood will be a sign for you on the houses where you are; and when I see the blood, I will pass over you. No destructive plague will touch you when I strike Egypt. (Exodus 12:12-13)

The Israelites obeyed these commands. By faith, they placed the blood of a perfect lamb on their doorframes. At midnight, the Lord struck down all the firstborn of Egypt, but the firstborn of the Israelites survived. God "passed over" the Israelites because of the blood on their doorframes.

By Faith The Israelites Followed The Passover Requirements

By faith Moses instructed the Hebrews to follow God's Passover requirements. By faith the Israelites did as God commanded (see Exodus 12:28). There was no power in the blood to stop death. It was simply the blood of a year old lamb. By faith, when the Israelites sprinkled the blood on their doors, death bypassed them. Death passed over the Israelites because they obediently followed God's directions. Their visible action proved their faith.

A lamb had to be killed to protect the Israelites from God's wrath. By faith the Israelites performed the Passover sacrifice. The blood of a perfect lamb saved the Israelites from destruction in Egypt.

Jesus Is The Lamb Of God

The Passover sacrifice foreshadows the blood of Jesus, the ultimate Passover sacrifice. In the Old Testament, God accepted the blood from an animal sacrifice as a substitute for human sin. Blood was required to pay the penalty for sin because without the shedding of blood there can be no forgiveness (see Hebrews 9:22). These sacrifices were strictly symbolic. It is impossible for the blood of bulls and goats to take away sins (see Hebrews 10:4). That is why you need a Savior. Jesus is the Savior of the world (see 1 John 4:14).

Isaiah prophesied the Messiah would be slaughtered like a lamb (see Isaiah 53:7). Christ is our Passover lamb (see 1 Corinthians 5:7). Jesus is the "Lamb of God, who takes away the sin of the world!" (see John 1:29). Jesus, God's perfect son, came to be the final blood sacrifice. Because of Jesus, animal sacrifice is no longer necessary. Jesus paid the price, once for all (see Hebrews 9:12)...for all who believe in Him.

Sin carries a very high price tag, but you do not have to pay it. Jesus was your substitute. He gave His blood so that you would not have to. To receive the benefit, you must do your part and trust Him by faith. Just as the Israelites sacrificed their Passover lambs by faith, you must accept Jesus, your Passover lamb, by faith. Salvation is obtained by faith alone. Faith is the only way to be spared from God's wrath.

The Lord's Supper—To Remember Jesus' Sacrifice For Sin

When God initiated the Passover, He told the Israelites that it was to be an annual commemoration of how God delivered the Hebrews from Egypt. Each year the Israelites were to thank God for saving them from the plague of death and delivering them from slavery and sin. The Jews obeyed God and continue to keep this celebration to this day. In New Testament times, many gathered in Jerusalem for the Passover. Interestingly, Jesus was crucified during one of the Passover celebrations.

Just before He died, Jesus celebrated the Passover with His disciples. When they were finished, Jesus introduced the Lord's Supper, which He told His disciples to do in remembrance of Him. Jesus gave each disciple bread, which was symbolic of His body that would be given. Then Jesus gave them wine, which symbolized His blood, that would pour out as a sacrifice.

The purpose of the Lord's Supper is to remember what God has done. The next time you have the opportunity to participate in a Lord's Supper service, I pray you will do so with a joyous and thankful heart, remembering the great sacrifice that Jesus made. Yes, my friends, there is power in the blood. The power of forgiveness is found in the blood of Jesus Christ, which was shed on the cross just for you.

Strengthen Your Faith

What were the Israelites commanded to do in order to save their firstborn?

What type of animal were the Israelites asked to slaughter during the first Passover?

According to Hebrews 9:12, what was required of Jesus in order to provide eternal redemption?

Meditate on the "blood of the lamb" by reading Hebrews 9:22, Isaiah 53:7, 1 Corinthians 5:7, and John 1:29.

29

GOD'S PROTECTION

> *By faith the people passed through the Red Sea as on dry land; but when the Egyptians tried to do so, they were drowned.*
> (Hebrews 11:29)

In our playroom at home, I believe we have close to a hundred children's videos. Although I bought them for my children, there are a few that I enjoy as much as they do. One such movie is *The Lion King*. My favorite part of that movie is when Simba goes into the land of the hyenas against his father's wishes.

In that scene, the hyenas see Simba enter their territory and quickly surround him. Little Simba growls at the hyenas in an attempt to frighten them away, but the hyenas are unimpressed. As the hyenas begin moving in for the kill, Simba continues to growl at them, but his feeble attempts at strength only embolden the hyenas.

Just as they are about to pounce on Simba, the hyenas hear a thunderous roar. When they look up, they see that Mufasa, Simba's father, has arrived. The hyenas realize that the balance of power has shifted and quickly run away. Simba learns that protection and deliverance comes when he is in the presence of his father.

Crossing The Red Sea

Today's story has been called the greatest miracle in the Bible. The Israelites were slaves in the land of Egypt. Moses spoke to Pharaoh time and time again, yet he refused to let God's people go. Following the tenth plague, which killed all the firstborn of Egypt, Pharaoh ordered Moses and all the Israelites to leave the country. As they left, the Israelites plundered the Egyptians, taking with them gold, silver and clothing.

They loaded up all of their possessions and headed toward the Promised Land. It must have been the happiest day of their lives. They were free! After four hundred years of slavery, God kept His promise and set them free. Moses was the great deliverer, who had the courage to stand up to Pharaoh and speak on their behalf. Life couldn't get much better for the Israelites.

Everything was fine…until Pharaoh changed his mind. The pharaoh decided he did not want to lose all of his slave labor, so he began to chase the Israelites. When the Israelites saw the Egyptians coming after them, they were filled with fear. They immediately turned to Moses and complained. Moses demonstrated his faith when he said,

> "Do not be afraid. Stand firm and you will see the deliverance the LORD will bring you today. The Egyptians you see today you will never see again. The LORD will fight for you; you need only to be still." (Exodus 14:13-14)

What happened next was nothing short of miraculous. God commanded Moses to raise his staff and stretch his hand over the Red Sea (see Exodus 14:16). Moses obeyed. God caused a strong east wind to divide the water, so the Israelites could cross through the sea on dry ground (see Exodus 14:21-22). When the Israelites were safely across the Red Sea, God again commanded Moses to stretch his hand over the Red Sea. This time the waters flowed back over the Egyptians, and they were all killed (see Exodus 14:26-28).

The Power Of God's Protection

Have you ever wondered why God protected the Israelites but not the Egyptians? I know I have. I believe God protected the Israelites because they knew Him. The Israelites had a relationship with God. They were His people. They lived by faith and God placed them under His protection. God was with them at all times…even when they grumbled and complained.

The Egyptians, on the other hand, did not know God (see Exodus 5:2). They had no relationship with Him. The Egyptians did not live by faith. Instead, they placed their trust in themselves and almighty Egypt. Their lack of faith proved fatal.

When our family prepared to move to Las Vegas, many people expressed concerns about our safety. One well-meaning friend said, "Don't you know all the evil influences that can consume your children? Don't you know how dangerous it is to live in a city like Las Vegas? Clinton, MS is a much better place to raise a family!" I know her words were spoken out of love, but they were not words of faith. The truth is, we are safer in Las Vegas, in the will of God, than we would be anywhere else in the world, outside the will of God. God protects those who live by faith.

The Bible records many examples of God's protection and deliverance. One of my favorites involves the prophet Elisha. In 2 Kings, chapter 6, the king of Aram was intent on capturing Elisha. The king's intelligence indicated that Elisha was in Dothan. So the king sent his army to surround the city. Elisha's servant saw that they were surrounded and asked what they should do. Do you remember Elisha's response?

> "Don't be afraid," the prophet answered. "Those who are with us are more than those who are with them." And Elisha prayed, "O Lord, open his eyes so he may see." (2 Kings 6:16-17)

God answered Elisha's prayer. The Lord opened the servant's eyes and he saw that the hills were full of horses and chariots of fire. The servant realized he had nothing to fear because God's heavenly army was protecting them.

Isaiah 43:1-4 is a beautiful passage of Scripture, which demonstrates how God protects those who have placed their trust in Him.

> "Don't be afraid, I've redeemed you. I've called your name. You're mine. When you're in over your head, I'll be there with you. When you're in rough waters, you will not go down. When you're between a rock and a hard place, it won't be a dead end—because I am God, your personal God, the Holy of Israel, your Savior. I paid a huge price for you: all of Egypt, with rich Cush and Seba thrown in! *That's how much you mean to me!* *That's* how much I love you! I'd sell off the whole world to get you back, trade the creation just for you." (Isaiah 43:1-4 MSG)

I don't know what your situation is today. Your marriage may be in turmoil. Your finances may be a mess. Your health may be failing. The good news is you are not alone. God is with you.

God loves you. He's watching over you, and promises to protect you in your time of need. If you place your trust in Him, and live by faith, God will do for you what He did for the Israelites. He will divide the sea, and you will learn first hand that protection and deliverance come when you live by faith in the presence of God.

Strengthen Your Faith

What circumstances cause you anxiety or fear?

How do you think the Israelites felt when they saw the Egyptians approaching?

How do you think the Israelites felt when the Red Sea miraculously opened before them?

Meditate on Isaiah 43:1-4. Thank God for His constant protection.

30

YOUR WAY OR GOD'S WAY

By faith the walls of Jericho fell, after the people had marched around them for seven days.
(Hebrews 11:30)

I have never been very good at reading instructions. A few years ago, I went to a department store to buy a baby crib. After I showed the salesman the crib I wanted, he said he would help load it onto my truck. When I pulled around to the back of the store, the salesman prepared to place a large box in the back of my truck. I said, "Sir, I wanted the baby crib I showed you in the store. I don't want a box." The salesman informed me that the one I wanted was not for sale; it was only a display model. He said all cribs come unassembled, but the store would be happy to assemble mine for an additional fee of only $25.

I chose not to give the store any more of my money. I brought the box home and began the daunting task of putting together the baby crib. I took a brief look at the instructions, which were written in every language except English, and decided just to wing it. After all, how hard could it be? It was only a baby crib.

Four hours later, our crib was finished, and it looked pathetic. It was uneven, unstable, and bore little resemblance to the picture on the box. Worst of all, there were ten pieces left over, and I had no idea where they went. I tried to convince my wife that this crib would work just fine for our firstborn child, but one look in her eyes told me exactly what I needed to do. I loaded up the crib, went back to the department store, and paid the $25 to have it assembled. It was the best $25 I spent that year!

I don't know why I refuse to follow instructions. I should have learned by now that when I do my own thing, I make a big mess; but when I carefully follow the instructions, I am pleased with the end result. I believe my pride causes me to think I am smarter than the author of the instructions. As I grow older, I am learning that I save both time and money when I follow the instructions.

The Christian life is much the same way. God has provided the greatest instruction manual in the world—His Word. It provides a detailed account of how you are to live. If you follow the instructions completely, God promises success.

You must choose how you will live. You can live your way, or you can live God's way. You can follow the instructions in the Bible, or you can try and make a go of it on your own. But remember, the journey of faith is not an a la carte menu. You cannot choose to obey God's instructions in one area of your life and ignore them in another. That is not living by faith.

You know you live by faith when you follow God's instructions completely. Even when you don't understand. Even when you think you can do it better on your own. Even when God's instructions don't make sense to you. Your complete obedience proves that you believe God's way is better than your way.

<u>The Consequences Of Unbelief</u>

After the Israelites passed through the Red Sea, they continued their journey toward the land of Canaan. When they reached the border of the Promised Land, twelve spies were sent out to explore Canaan. The spies reported Canaan to be a land of abundance that was heavily fortified. Ten of the spies exaggerated the extent of the challenge ahead. Only Caleb and Joshua believed the Israelites could take the land with God's help. Joshua and Caleb implored the people not to fear and rebel against God. But the bad report spread like wildfire throughout the camp (see Numbers 13).

The people gossiped and chose to listen to negative talk. The Israelites rebelled against God, and threatened to stone Moses, Aaron, Joshua, and Caleb. God was angered by their lack of faith, and refused to allow the older generation of Israelites to enter the Promised Land, except for Joshua and Caleb (see Numbers 14).

Forty years passed between the events of Hebrews 11:29 (the parting of the Red Sea), and the events of Hebrews 11:30 (the walls of Jericho). This time period is skipped because it cannot be used to demonstrate the faith of the Israelites.

When Moses died, Joshua was chosen to lead God's people (see Joshua 1:1). He was chosen because of his faith. Joshua had trusted God during the initial exploration of the Promised Land forty years prior. When God called Joshua as the leader, He promised to be with him, and told Joshua he must be strong and courageous (see Joshua 1:5-9).

Before the Israelites could conquer Jericho, they had to cross the Jordan River. The Israelites crossed the Jordan River by faith. God miraculously stopped the waters of the Jordan River, and the Israelites crossed on dry ground. Because of their faith, God's power was again visible (see Joshua 3).

The Battle Of Jericho

The commander of the Lord's army appeared to Joshua and said that Jericho was already delivered into his hands. Joshua was given detailed instructions for the attack. The Israelites were to march around the city once a day, for six consecutive days. Seven priests blowing trumpets were to lead out in front of the ark. Some of the armed men were to march in front of the seven priests, and some were to march behind the ark. No one was to say a word. On the seventh day, they were to march around Jericho seven times, as the priests blew their trumpets. When the priests sounded a long blast on their trumpets, all of the people were to shout. The walls of Jericho would then collapse, enabling the Israelites to easily enter the city.

By faith, the Israelites circled Jericho just as God commanded. On the seventh day, when Joshua heard the long trumpet blast, he commanded, "Shout! For the LORD has given you the city!" (Joshua 6:16). The people shouted and the walls collapsed. Every man charged in and took the city of Jericho. They devoted the city to God (see Joshua 6).

Jericho Was Conquered By Faith

Jericho was the first obstacle encountered in taking the Promised Land. It was one of the oldest cities in the world and was a symbol of military power. It was located at the mouth of the Jordan River. Its walls were enormous (25 feet high and 20 feet thick) and highly fortified. Guards could see the surrounding territory very well.

By faith, the Israelites followed God's instructions exactly as they were given. Amazingly, there is no record of any doubts or grumbling in Joshua 6. God's plan seemed absurd on the surface. They could have said, "This is ridiculous. We will look like complete idiots walking around in a circle each day. What good can a march do, anyway? Let's show them how tough we really are!"

But the Israelites had finally realized that God's way was

better than their way. When Joshua told the people God's plan, they marched. No discussion. By faith the walls fell down. It was an amazing display of God's power to both the Israelites, and the inhabitants of Canaan.

Faith Makes A Difference

When the Israelites were poised to take the Promised Land the first time, a bad report spread like wildfire through the camp. Moses encouraged the people not to be afraid. Moses told the people that God would go ahead and fight for them just as He did in Egypt. The people chose not to trust the Lord (see Deuteronomy 1:29-33).

They made the decision to live their way and not God's way, and the results were disastrous. Every Israelite, who was at least twenty years old at the time the spies gave their report, died wandering around in the desert (except Joshua and Caleb). They did not receive the land God promised, because without faith it is impossible to please God (see Hebrews 11:6).

Joshua and the next generation of Israelites were given very specific instructions on how to conquer the city of Jericho. Although the instructions made no sense from a military standpoint, the people followed them, down to the smallest detail.

By faith, the Israelites chose to live God's way instead of their way. As a result, they witnessed a tremendous display of God's power, as the walls of Jericho miraculously fell. Their victory was assured because God was in control.

Your Way Or God's Way

God's way is always better than your way. God loves you and knows what is best for you. The Bible is your personal instruction book for daily living. Make a commitment each day to follow His instructions completely. Show God that you believe His way is better than your way.

Strengthen Your Faith

How specific are you when it comes to following a recipe or an instruction manual?

What specific instructions did God give to the Israelites at the battle of Jericho?

Why did it require faith for the Israelites to follow God's instructions?

In what area of your life do you need to follow God's instructions completely? Talk to Him about it today.

31

CAN GOD USE YOU?

*By faith the prostitute Rahab, because she
welcomed the spies, was not killed
with those who were disobedient.*
(Hebrews 11:31)

As you progress on your journey of faith, you will be faced with opportunities to be used by God. When the time comes, you may feel you are unworthy. Satan will bring up your past, and remind you of all the bad things you've done. He will try to convince you that God could never use anyone like you. If Satan is able to persuade you that God can't use you, he has accomplished his task.

I don't know how bad of a sinner you are. I know nothing about your "past" or the skeletons in your closet. I don't have a copy of your rap sheet or your criminal history. But one thing I do know: Jesus Christ died on the cross for *all* sinners. If you have been touched by Jesus, then you are a person of extreme value to God.

God specializes in taking sinners and turning them into servants. Abraham lied and gave his wife to another man. Jacob was a deceiver. Joseph was a dreamer. Moses was a murderer. David was an adulterer. Peter was a coward. Paul arrested and persecuted Christians. These men all shared a common bond: they failed God. Through their failures, God touched them and changed them. Once transformed, they became great vessels, which God used mightily for His kingdom.

The Story Of Rahab The Prostitute

Prior to the invasion, Joshua sent two spies on a reconnaissance mission of Jericho and the surrounding countryside. The spies went and stayed at the house of a prostitute named Rahab. Rahab hid the spies under some flax on the roof of her house. The king of Jericho found out the spies had gone to Rahab's house, and he ordered Rahab to send out the spies. Rahab admitted the men had come to her, but said she did not know anything about them. She lied and said the men left at dusk, when it was time to close the city gate. The king's men immediately left the city in search of the spies (see Joshua 2:1-7).

After the pursuers left, Rahab went to the roof and told the spies, "I know that the LORD has given this land to you…The LORD your God is God in heaven above and on the earth below" (Joshua 2:9, 11).

Rahab asked that her family be spared during the invasion, and because she had saved their lives, the spies agreed. The spies instructed Rahab to tie a red cord in her window and keep her entire family inside her house during the battle. As they prepared to leave Jericho, Rahab warned the spies to hide in the hills for three days before returning to their camp. The spies opened Rahab's window, and rappelled down the city's exterior wall. After hiding for three days, the spies reported to Joshua everything that had happened (see Joshua 2:12-24).

When the Israelites invaded Jericho, they burned the entire city. But Joshua spared Rahab and her family, and she went to live with the Israelites (see Joshua 6:24-25).

Rahab Is Saved By Faith And Used By God

Rahab was an unlikely ally for Israel. She was a prostitute, and a Gentile. But God, in His infinite wisdom, directed the spies to Rahab's house.

Because Rahab was a prostitute, it was common for strange men to frequent her home at all hours. This enabled the spies to blend in with their surroundings. Rahab's home was also strategically located along the city wall, which God used as an escape route for the spies. Most importantly, God knew Rahab's heart was open to Him.

Rahab, a Gentile prostitute, was saved by faith. In Joshua 2:11, Rahab declared, "The LORD your God is God in heaven above and on the earth below." She exemplifies how salvation by faith was possible for *all* people, even in the Old Testament. God's grace was available to Rahab, just as it was for the Israelites.

Rahab put her faith to work when she hid the spies, and facilitated their escape from Jericho. Rahab's actions proved her faith in God to be genuine. James 2:25 says, "Rahab the prostitute [was] considered righteous for what she did when she gave lodging to the spies and sent them off in a different direction."

God rewarded Rahab for her faith. God spared her life during the destruction of Jericho. Rahab also received a fresh start in life. She lived with the Israelites, married a man named Salmon, and gave birth to a son named Boaz (who later married Ruth). Rahab, a former prostitute now redeemed by God, was the great-great-grandmother of King David (see Matthew 1:5-6), and ultimately related to Jesus Christ, the King of Kings (see Matthew 1:16).

Repentance

Repentance is defined as "a turning away from sin, disobedience, or rebellion and a turning back to God."[1] True repentance occurs when you are genuinely sorry for your sin. When you repent, you literally turn your life around and go in the opposite direction. True repentance is a godly sorrow (see 2 Corinthians 7:10), which causes a change in your behavior. *When you experience godly sorrow, you deeply regret your sin and turn from it.* Few people exhibit godly sorrow and repent of their sin.

The opposite of godly sorrow is worldly sorrow. Worldly sorrow is prevalent. However, it does not result in true repentance. Worldly sorrow is nothing more than a façade, because it does not bring about a corresponding change in behavior. It is merely regret over the *consequences* of your sin. *When you experience worldly sorrow, you regret getting caught.*

For example, a teenage girl can experience either godly or worldly sorrow when she is caught sneaking out of her house late at night to meet her boyfriend. It is godly sorrow if she turns from this behavior, and never sneaks out again. However, it is worldly sorrow if she returns to her previous behavior the minute her punishment is lifted.

Genuine Faith Requires Repentance

Repentance and faith are closely related. You cannot have one without the other. When you repent, you turn away from sin. You give up your old lifestyle. By faith, you turn to God. You give God control of your life and choose to live His way.

God chooses to use the lowly, and the despised (see 1 Corinthians 1:28) for His purpose. "Lowly" and "despised" aptly describes Rahab's former life as a prostitute. By faith, Rahab turned to God, and placed her trust in Him. She felt godly sorrow for her past actions, turned her life around and went in the opposite direction. She made a clean break from her past lifestyle, and no longer made her living as a prostitute. She chose to live God's way with God's chosen people, and because of her faith was blessed to be an ancestor of the Messiah.

Changed By God

There may be sins in your life, which hinder your ability to live by faith. Choose to purify yourself of everything that contaminates your body and spirit. Instead, perfect holiness (see 2 Corinthians 7:1). When you repent from sin, and live by faith, you will be amazed at how God uses you for His purpose.

Strengthen Your Faith

What are some reasons why you feel God can't use you?

What did Abraham, Moses, David, and Rahab have in common?

Why do you think God uses sinners to accomplish His work on the earth?

In what area of service do you feel God wants to use you? Make yourself available to Him today.

32

MODERN-DAY IDOLS

And what more shall I say? I do not have time to tell about Gideon, Barak, Samson, Jephthah, David, Samuel and the prophets, who through faith conquered kingdoms, administered justice, and gained what was promised; who shut the mouths of lions, quenched the fury of the flames, and escaped the edge of the sword; whose weakness was turned to strength; and who became powerful in battle and routed foreign armies.
(Hebrews 11:32-34)

The reality show "American Idol" has become one of the most popular shows on network television. I understand that literally hundreds of thousands of people audition, hoping to become the next "American Idol." The auditions are narrowed down to a final group of twenty-five contestants. These finalists go on television, and are judged by the viewing public, to see who will win a national recording contract and the adoration of millions of people. When the winner is selected, he or she is pronounced to be the true "American Idol." It is amazing how quickly someone can rise from obscurity to become an "American Idol." I have come to the conclusion that idols come pretty cheap in today's culture.

As you continue on your journey of faith, you will most certainly struggle with the issue of idolatry. When most people hear the word idolatry, they think of people worshiping wooden poles or statues made of gold. This may have been the case in the Old Testament, but today, idolatry is much more subtle.

Idolatry During The Period Of The Judges

The Israelites served God while Joshua was alive, and during the time of the elders who outlived Joshua. After the elders died, a whole generation grew up, which neither knew the Lord nor what He had done (see Judges 2:10).

The judges were men and women who led Israel from the time of Joshua's death until the anointing of the first king. The period of the judges was from 1380-1050 BC. During this time, Israel was a loose alliance of twelve tribes. There was no king or strong religious leader to hold the tribes together. It was a time where "everyone did as he saw fit" (Judges 21:25).

Gideon, Samson, Jephthah, and Samuel were judges. Barak lived during the time of the judges. These men were mentioned in Hebrews 11:32 because they lived by faith. But for most of the people who lived during this time, faith was noticeably absent.

Throughout this period, the Israelites did evil in the eyes of the Lord. Judges 3:7 clarifies this evil: "They forgot the LORD their God and served the Baals and the Asherahs." Baal was the most-worshiped of the many Canaanite gods and goddesses. Baal was the nature and fertility god. Asherah was the wife of El, or sometimes Baal, in Canaanite mythology. Women loved to worship Asherah.

When Israel turned its back on God, He was angered. He handed Israel over to its enemies. Periodically, God would rise up judges to save the Israelites. They would listen to the judge as long as he/she lived, but quickly return to idol worship as soon as the judge died. This cycle of sin-punishment-repentance-deliverance occurs seven times in the book of Judges.

Definition Of Idolatry

Idolatry is the worship of other gods. It is worshiping created things rather than the Creator (see Romans 1:25). Idolatry is a sin (see Galatians 5:20). When God gave Moses the Ten Commandments, two of them dealt specifically with idolatry:

"You shall have no other gods before me" (Exodus 20:3).
"You shall not make for yourself an idol" (Exodus 20:4).

God listed these two commandments first and placed heavy emphasis on them, because He knew it was hard for the Israelites to place their faith in God alone. In the Old Testament, idolatry was a constant problem. It primarily involved the worship of pagan mythological gods. These gods were often depicted in the form of statues. The period of the judges was marked by repeated cycles of idolatry, as the people chose to worship Baal and Asherah over God.

In the New Testament, Jesus put His own spin on these commandments:

"Worship the Lord your God, and serve him only" (see Matthew 4:10).
"No servant can serve two masters" (see Luke 16:13).

The New Testament definition of idolatry shifts away from a focus on physical statues to a much broader definition. Today, idolatry is anything, which a worshiper values more highly than God. An idol is any thing or person, which takes first place in your life. Idolatry can include your car, house, job, loved ones, pride, fame, etc.

The most dangerous aspect of modern-day idolatry is its subtle nature. You can go through the motions of Christian worship, and all the while your heart is devoted to something else.

Even Good Things Can Become Idols

I don't struggle very much with the "evil" things of the world; it's the "acceptable" things that give me trouble. It isn't difficult for me to say "no" to stealing, fraud, or murder. However, I have a very hard time saying "no" to envy, success, and wanting more "things" in life.

I have learned that you can make an idol out of just about anything. Success, money, fame, your house, your yard, your job, even another person can be your idol. There is nothing wrong with any of these things, until you place them ahead of God. Good things become bad things when they take your focus off of the best thing. Don't let the good things of this world rob you of the best thing, which is your personal relationship with Jesus Christ.

Celebrity Worship

We live in a culture that promotes the worship of other people. We even refer to them as idols. A couple of years ago, as my family walked through the mall, we saw a large group of people rush to the entrance of a music store. When I asked what was happening, someone told me that Michael Jackson was inside the store. Hundreds of people were waiting just to catch a glimpse of their idol.

My family recently went to see an Elvis Presley impersonator at the Las Vegas Hilton. During the performance, "Elvis" took his scarf, wiped the perspiration from his face, and then tossed it out into the crowd. The audience went wild. Women actually began lining up along the front of the stage, as "Elvis" threw out additional sweat-soaked scarves. As I looked on at this unbelievable scene, I said to my wife, "Don't they know that's not him?" (Unfortunately, my wife didn't hear me because she had run to the stage!)

It may be Elvis, Michael Jackson, Kobe Bryant or Brittany Spears. Unfortunately, we have placed people on a pedestal and turned them into idols. We worship them with our money, our time, and the devotion of our hearts. Why is it that we worship people instead of God?

God Alone Is Worthy To Be Worshiped

You were created with an inbuilt need to worship. You will worship something. Satan's goal is to keep you from worshiping God. He offers a wide variety of people and things for you to worship in place of God. But these are all very small gods.

Please remember that God alone is worthy to be worshiped. The Bible is clear that God is to be exalted above all gods (see Psalm 97:9) and people (see Psalm 99:2 AB). The gods of the nations are idols (see Psalm 96:5). God is to be feared above all gods (see Psalm 96:4).

True worship focuses on God. Because Jesus is God in human form, your worship must also include Jesus. This is a crucial point. If you deny Jesus, you have not worshiped the one true God. You have worshiped an idol.

Be On Your Guard Against Idolatry

Idolatry was the Israelites greatest temptation, and can easily be yours as well. Idolatry is often subtle. You must constantly be on your guard to let nothing come between you and God.

1 John 5:21 says, "Dear children, keep yourselves from idols." God and God alone is to be worshiped. Take whatever steps are necessary to be sure that no thing or person is more important to you than God.

Strengthen Your Faith

What comes to mind when you think about idols?

What is the New Testament definition of idolatry?

What are some areas in your life, which compete with God for first place?

Meditate on Matthew 6:33. Pray and make a commitment to seek first the kingdom of God.

33

THE POWER OF THE HOLY SPIRIT

And what more shall I say? I do not have time to tell about Gideon, Barak, Samson, Jephthah, David, Samuel and the prophets, who through faith conquered kingdoms, administered justice, and gained what was promised; who shut the mouths of lions, quenched the fury of the flames, and escaped the edge of the sword; whose weakness was turned to strength; and who became powerful in battle and routed foreign armies.
(Hebrews 11:32-34)

Have you ever gone out to your car and discovered that the battery was dead? The only way to start your car in this situation is with a set of jumper cables. Jumper cables are relatively easy to use. You hook one side of the cables to the dead battery, and the other side to a good battery. When you turn the key, the good battery provides power to the dead battery, enabling you to start your car.

As a teenager, I had a car with a weak battery. I asked my parents for a new battery one Christmas. Instead, they gave me a set of jumper cables! Although I was disappointed at first, those jumper cables have helped me numerous times over the years, by facilitating the transfer of power from someone else's car to my own.

This is similar to the role of the Holy Spirit. The Holy Spirit has the ability to connect you to God. He can transfer power from God to help you in your Christian life. Too many Christians rely on their own strength and do not allow the Holy Spirit to help them. These Christians are just like the battery of my old car. They are weak and ineffective. They need the power that is found in the Holy Spirit of God.

The Spirit Of God In The Old Testament

Throughout the Old Testament, the Spirit of the Lord came upon selected individuals and empowered them. The Spirit of God came upon a person in power (see 1 Samuel 10:10; 1 Samuel 16:13). The Spirit enabled a person to do God's will or to serve God in some special way.

Sometimes the Spirit of God remained with that person throughout their lifetime (e.g. Samuel and David). Other times, the Spirit was given for a specific task or period of time, and then departed. The Spirit of God came upon Saul in power (see 1 Samuel 10:10), and later departed (see 1 Samuel 16:14) because God rejected Saul as king.

The Spirit of God was upon the men listed in Hebrews 11:32: David (see 1 Samuel 16:13), Gideon (see Judges 6:34), Samson (see Judges 13:25), and Jephthah (see Judges 11:29).

These men conquered their enemies, administered justice among the Israelites, and gained what was promised. They were able to kill ferocious animals with their bare hands, and withstand heat from resistance to a prophetic message. God used their weaknesses as an opportunity to showcase His power and glory. All of this was done by faith, through God's power.

The Holy Spirit In The New Testament

The Spirit of God in the Old Testament is the same person as the Holy Spirit in the New Testament. The Holy Spirit is the third person of the Trinity. He is Holy because He is God, and Spirit, because He is invisible. The Holy Spirit was not given until after Jesus ascended into Heaven. Jesus promised that, although He was leaving, He would send the Spirit to be with you forever (see John 14:16-17).

When you accept Jesus as your Savior, you are "born again," by the Spirit (see John 3:3, 5-6). At the moment of your salvation, you are baptized with the Holy Spirit, which means the Spirit of God comes to live within you. From that time forward, you are indwelled by the Holy Spirit. The Spirit lives permanently inside of you for the remainder of your time on the earth. This is a change from the Old Testament, where the Spirit was only given to selected believers, and could later be taken away.

The Promise Of Greater Power

Jesus said, "I tell you the truth, anyone who has faith in me will do what I have been doing. He will do even greater things than these, because I am going to the Father" (John 14:12). Jesus is God in human form. How could anyone do greater things than Jesus?

God's plan for salvation required that Jesus live and die as a man. He was subjected to the limitations of a human body, and therefore had no power of His own. The power that Jesus exhibited during His earthly ministry was from the Holy Spirit.

Just like you, Jesus could only be in one place at a time during His earthly ministry. The greater power that Jesus refers to comes from the indwelling Holy Spirit. The Spirit indwells believers all across the world. This provides Him an opportunity to work through many different people at the same time. The Holy Spirit can simultaneously use people for His purposes in Las Vegas, New York City, Sydney, Tokyo, Paris, and Buenos Aires.

The Purpose Of The Holy Spirit—Power To Build God's Kingdom

Jesus told His disciples, "But you will receive power when the Holy Spirit comes on you; and you will be my witnesses in Jerusalem, and in all Judea and Samaria, and to the ends of the earth" (Acts 1:8).

God's plan is to use His church to spread the news of Jesus throughout the world. This can only be accomplished through the power of the Holy Spirit. The Holy Spirit was given to equip you for your role in God's plan. He provides *everything* you need to fulfill whatever God has called you to do.

Today, power from the Holy Spirit does not refer to extraordinary strength, such as Samson had, or the ability to perform the miraculous. Holy Spirit power enables your work for God to yield extraordinary results.

Holy Spirit power gives you the ability to speak boldly, when you would rather remain silent. It provides the courage to stand up for your beliefs when they are attacked by the world. The Holy Spirit supplies the confidence needed to start and complete a task, which you know is beyond your own natural abilities. The Spirit gives you insight into the Scriptures and the world around you.

By Faith, Allow God's Power To Flow Through You

I recently returned home from a mission trip and discovered that my kitchen faucet was leaking. Prompt action was needed to prevent water damage, so I called a plumber. He quickly came out to the house and replaced the faucet.

Later that evening, when my wife attempted to run the dishwasher, she found that it wouldn't start. In fact, when Lisa set the wash cycle, it didn't even make a sound. There was no way I was going to repair the dishwasher. I had put over $200 into it less than six months ago. I could feel my frustration level rising. I had just purchased a new faucet and now I needed to replace the dishwasher as well!

The following day, Lisa and I picked out a brand new dishwasher for our home. To help us save money, a dear friend offered to install it free of charge. When he arrived at our house, Manny said the first thing he needed to do was pull out the old dishwasher. So he climbed under the sink to see how it was connected. A few seconds later, he pulled himself out of the cabinet and said, "Do you know that your dishwasher is not plugged in?"

Manny plugged the dishwasher into the electrical outlet, and the wash cycle started immediately. We realized that the plumber had unplugged the dishwasher while he was working on the sink and had simply forgotten to plug it back in when he was finished. The dishwasher wasn't broken; it just needed to be plugged into the power source! Once it was plugged in, the dishwasher worked just fine.

Many Christians are like this dishwasher. When you become a Christian, you are given a new nature. Sometimes this new nature does not work the way you think it should. You feel weak and wonder why you are having such a tough time. That is why you need to understand the power of the Holy Spirit. Just like the dishwasher is dependent on electricity for power, Christians are dependent on the Holy Spirit for power. The Holy Spirit provides the power that enables you to function properly as a Christian.

The Bible commands you to live by faith, just as these heroes did in the Old Testament. By faith, God's power is available to you, through the Holy Spirit. The choice is up to you. You can live each day depending on your own power and strength, or you can plug into the power source of God through the Holy Spirit. When you daily seek God with all of your heart and ask Him to direct your paths, He will give you the strength and the power to do great things for the kingdom of God.

Strengthen Your Faith

Why do some people not want to talk about the Holy Spirit?

How did the Holy Spirit work in the Old Testament?

How does the Holy Spirit work today?

How does the Holy Spirit work in you?

34

ORDINARY PEOPLE

> *And what more shall I say? I do not have time to tell about Gideon, Barak, Samson, Jephthah, David, Samuel and the prophets, who through faith conquered kingdoms, administered justice, and gained what was promised; who shut the mouths of lions, quenched the fury of the flames, and escaped the edge of the sword; whose weakness was turned to strength; and who became powerful in battle and routed foreign armies.*
> (Hebrews 11:32-34)

I believe God calls ordinary people to do extra-ordinary things. When ordinary people accept the challenge of God, they become extra-ordinary. People often think that they are not talented enough to serve God. Some people think they are not smart enough to be used by Him. Others have shared with me they don't feel spiritually mature enough to tell someone about God.

The result of these negative thought patterns is that many people just sit on the sidelines. They do not receive the blessings, which come from doing great things for the kingdom of God. Why? Because they bought into Satan's lie that they are not qualified to make a difference.

The men listed in Hebrews 11:32 lived for God, and God was with them. By faith these, and countless more unnamed individuals throughout the Bible, were empowered by the Spirit of God. God's faithful servants accomplished things beyond their own limited abilities. They conquered their enemies, administered justice among the Israelites, and gained what was promised. They were able to kill ferocious animals with their bare hands, and withstand heat from resistance to a prophetic message.

<u>The Story Of Gideon</u>

Gideon was an ordinary man in every sense of the word. He was a farmer when the angel of the Lord appeared to him and said, "The LORD is with you, mighty warrior" (Judges 6:12). Gideon was called to save Israel from the Midianites. He had no experience as a warrior. Because of this, Gideon questioned how he could save Israel. God promised to be with Gideon, and they would strike down the Midianites together.

Gideon felt insecure. He knew he was not qualified to lead Israel in a military campaign. He questioned that God was really speaking to him, and so he requested a sign. Gideon prepared God an offering and placed it on a rock. The angel of the Lord touched the offering with his staff and it was consumed by fire. Gideon realized he had seen the angel of the Lord and feared for his life. God reassured Gideon that he would not die. This story provides one of the names by which God reveals himself. God is Jehovah Shalom, "The Lord is Peace" (see Judges 6:17-24).

The Spirit of the Lord came upon Gideon, and he sent out a call for volunteers. He began to experience feelings of inadequacy, and so he asked God for two signs. Gideon placed a piece of wool fleece on the floor. For the first sign, Gideon asked God to place dew on the wool, but leave the ground dry. And that is what happened. The next day, Gideon asked God not to be angry, but to allow him one more request. Gideon reversed the test. He asked God to keep the fleece dry and the ground surrounding it wet. And God did so.

Gideon gathered 32,000 men to fight, but God felt that number was too large. Such a large fighting force would enable Israel to boast that they defeated Midian in their own strength. God told Gideon that any men who were fearful were free to leave. 22,000 men left, and only 10,000 remained. God then cut Gideon's fighting force to a mere 300 men based on how they drank water. He chose the men who lapped with their hands to their mouths, because they were always alert to what was going on around them. Men who knelt to drink were sent home. God promised victory over the Midianites with the 300 men.

Just before the battle, God provided Gideon further assurance of His plan to use him to defeat the Midianites. Gideon and his servant, Purah, snuck down to the Midianite camp and overheard two men talking. One man dreamt a round loaf of barley bread came tumbling into the camp, where it overturned and collapsed a tent. The second man said that the bread was the sword of Gideon, and that God had given the camp into Gideon's hands. Gideon worshiped God and returned to camp (see Judges 7:9-15).

Gideon woke up his men and told them God had given the Midianite camp into their hands. He divided his men into three groups of 100. They had no weapons. Each man had only a trumpet and an empty jar with a torch inside. The purpose of the jar was to conceal the light of the torch. The men snuck up on the Midianites unnoticed, and fanned out around the camp. They blew their trumpets, and broke the jars, revealing the light from their torches. The men shouted, "A sword for the Lord and for Gideon!" God caused the Midianites to panic. Some turned and killed each other, and others ran away. Many who ran were captured or killed by allies from various tribes (see Judges 7:15-8:21).

Gideon was insecure and slow to be convinced of God's plan to use him. However, once he understood his purpose, he acted boldly. God commended him for his faith.

God Uses Ordinary People

Gideon was an ordinary man, a farmer. But he was used for an extraordinary purpose. God used Gideon to deliver Israel from the Midianites. Under his leadership, Israel enjoyed peace for forty years (see Judges 8:28).

Gideon's life illustrates an important truth: God uses ordinary people to do extraordinary things. God loves to take an ordinary person, who is completely devoted to Him, and do something extraordinary with them. The ordinary is made extraordinary by the power of the Holy Spirit.

How does God go about choosing His ordinary people? 1 Samuel 16:7b provides the answer: "The LORD does not look at the things man looks at. Man looks at the outward appearance, but the LORD looks at the heart." God does not care what you look like, or about your worldly qualifications (master's degree, ten years of work experience, etc.). God looks at your heart. He determines commitment by judging the heart.

I first saw this memo years ago. It provides a humorous example of how God chooses people differently than the world does. May it remind you that God uses ordinary people to do extra-ordinary things for His kingdom.

Memorandum

TO:
Jesus, Son of Joseph
Woodcrafter Carpenter Shop
Nazareth

FROM:
Jordan Management Consultants
Jerusalem

Dear Sir:

Thank you for submitting the resumes of the twelve men you have picked for management positions in your new organization. All of them have now taken our battery of tests; we have not only run the results through our computer, but also arranged personal interviews for each of them with our psychologist and vocational aptitude consultant.

It is the staff opinion that most of your nominees are lacking in background, education and vocational aptitude for the type of enterprise you are undertaking. They do not have the team concept. We would recommend that you continue your search for persons of experience in managerial ability and proven capability.

Simon Peter is emotionally unstable and given to fits of temper. Andrew has absolutely no qualities of leadership. The two brothers, James and John, the sons of Zebedee, place personal interest above company loyalty. Thomas demonstrates a questioning attitude that would tend to undermine morale.

We feel that it is our duty to tell you that Matthew has been blacklisted by the Greater Jerusalem Better Business Bureau. James, the son of Alphaeus, and Thaddaeus definitely have radical leanings, and they both registered a high score on the manic depressive scale.

One of the candidates, however, shows great potential. He is a man of ability and resourcefulness, meets people well, has a keen business mind and has contacts in high places. He is highly motivated, ambitious and responsible. We recommend Judas Iscariot as your controller and right-hand man. All of the other profiles are self-explanatory.

We wish you every success in your new venture.

Sincerely yours,

Jordan Management Consultants[1]

I have heard it said that, "God is not so much concerned with your ability, as He is with your availability" (source unknown). God looks for those whose hearts are fully committed to Him. He seeks those who are devoted to Him and willing to serve. These are the people God uses to demonstrate His power to the world.

<u>By Faith, Experience The Extraordinary Life</u>

God chooses to build His kingdom using ordinary people. His Holy Spirit provides the supernatural empowerment needed to get the job done. All God needs from you is a heart fully devoted to Him. By faith, trust Him with your life, and live beyond your capabilities. Watch God turn your ordinary life into something extraordinary.

Strengthen Your Faith

Why do you think God chooses to work through ordinary people?

How did God move Gideon from ordinary to extraordinary?

How does God choose the people He will use for extraordinary purpose?

Make yourself available to God. Ask Him to use you in such a way that it can only be explained by the power of God.

35

PRAYING IN FAITH

Women received back their dead, raised to life again. Others were tortured and refused to be released, so that they might gain a better resurrection.
(Hebrews 11:35)

A prayer offered in faith can do amazing things. Jeremiah Lamphier felt a burden for New York City. He wanted to see God move in the hearts of the people who lived there, so he began to pray. He printed up flyers announcing a Wednesday prayer meeting. On the first week, six people came to pray with him. On the second week, twenty people came. On the third week, forty people showed up to pray. In six months time, there were ten thousand people praying in faith that God would move in the city of New York.

This concerted prayer effort ushered in a time of great spiritual awakening. People from all across the city felt drawn to God. Thousands responded and were saved. Historians have called it the Prayer Revival of 1857. It all began with a man who prayed in faith.

Praying in faith can start a revival, save a marriage, or rescue a wayward child. Praying in faith can heal an illness, restore a relationship, or bring a financial miracle. Most people say that they believe in prayer. I say there is a big difference between believing in prayer and praying in faith.

Praying in faith goes back to our definition of faith in Hebrews 11:1 which says, "Now faith is being sure of what we hope for and certain of what we do not see." Praying in faith is more than wishful thinking. It is a confident expectation that God will respond to your prayer. If you doubt that God will answer, you show that your faith is weak.

Today's verse speaks of people who prayed, and how God responded to their prayers in miraculous ways. The prayer process starts with a problem in your life, which causes you to pray. As the size of your problem increases, so does the urge to pray. Pray for your needs. God cares and wants to intervene. Consider two classic examples from the Old Testament.

The Widow At Zarephath

During a drought, God told the prophet Elijah to go to Zarephath. When he got to town, he asked a widow to bring him some water, and a piece of bread. The widow said she had no bread. All she had was a handful of flour and a small amount of oil. Her plan was to use it to make a final meal for she and her son before they died. Elijah told the woman to make him a small cake of bread first, and then make something for she and her son to eat. Elijah promised the widow her flour and oil would last until the end of the drought. The widow did just as Elijah told her, and she never ran out of flour or oil (see 1 Kings 17:7-16).

Later, the widow's son became very sick and died. She accused Elijah of coming to convict her of sin and killing her son. Elijah took the boy up to his room. *He cried out to God* about the death of the widow's son. He stretched out on the boy and *asked God* three times to bring the boy back to life. God answered Elijah's prayer. The boy returned to life and Elijah carried him down to his mother. The widow told Elijah she was sure he spoke the word of the Lord (see 1 Kings 17:17-24, emphasis added).

The Shunammite's Son Restored To Life

Once when the prophet Elisha went to Shunem, a wealthy woman invited him to dinner. He started staying for a meal every time he was in town. The woman asked her husband to make a small room on the roof to provide Elisha a comfortable place to stay whenever he was in town. Elisha was grateful to the woman for all she had done and asked how he could return the favor. Although her husband was old and she had no son, the woman told Elisha she needed nothing. Elisha promised the woman she would have a son within the next year, and she did (see 2 Kings 4:8-17).

One day, when the son was out working with his father, he complained of a headache. The boy was sent home. He sat in his mother's lap and died later that day. The Shunammite woman laid her son on Elisha's bed, shut the door, and took off on her donkey to find Elisha. When she reached him at Mount Carmel, she grabbed his feet and asked why he caused her this pain by giving her a son just to take him away. Elisha sent his servant, Gehazi, ahead and told him to lay Elisha's staff on the boy's face. When Gehazi did this, the boy did not move. Gehazi reported to Elisha that the boy did not wake up. When Elisha reached the house, he went alone into the room with the boy and *prayed*. Then he stretched himself out on the boy. The boy's body grew warm. Elisha got up and paced the room. He returned to the bed and stretched out over the boy once again. The boy sneezed and opened his eyes. Elisha gave the Shunammite back her son (see 2 Kings 4:18-37, emphasis added).

God Works Through Prayer

Elijah raised the widow of Zarephath's son from the dead. In similar fashion, Elisha brought the Shunammite's son back from death. How were they able to do this? No, Elijah and Elisha were not endowed with magical powers. It was God's power that brought the boys back from death. But the prophets played an important role in this miracle. They prayed. And when the prophets prayed, God went to work. His power was revealed and God was glorified.

God wants you to realize your dependence upon Him, and so He works through the mechanism of prayer. Prayer is communicating with God. When you pray, you humble yourself before God, acknowledging that He alone has the power to handle any situation. It is through prayer that you gain access to the Holy Spirit's power.

Prayer is essential to your journey of faith, because it transports you from the physical world (where you live) into the spiritual realm (where God lives). The spiritual realm is beyond the laws of the physical universe, which means God is unlimited in what He can do.

God works through prayer. If you want to see God work in your life, you must pray, because it is through prayer that you gain access to the spiritual realm. In fact, God will do nothing until you pray (see James 4:2). Failure to pray is a sin (see 1 Samuel 12:23). It minimizes what God can do in your life.

Satan does not want you to pray. What you do in your own strength is of little consequence to him, because without God you can do nothing (see John 15:5). But he also knows that all things are possible with God (see Matthew 19:26). When you pray, you gain access to God's power, and that frightens him. Satan is willing to do whatever it takes to stop you from praying. He uses many different methods to keep you from prayer, but his favorite (and most effective) is busyness. Satan knows if he can keep you overworked, overscheduled, overburdened, and overtired, your prayer life will falter.

Jack Hayford, in his book *Prayer Is Invading the Impossible*, says, "Prayer can change anything. The impossible doesn't exist. His is the power. Ours is the prayer. Without Him, we cannot. Without us, He will not."[1]

God promises if you ask according to His will, He will hear your prayer and answer (see 1 John 5:14-15). Prayer is a faith issue. You must believe that your prayer will be answered (see Matthew 21:22). When you pray, God works.

Calling Out To God

Jeremiah 33:3 says, "Call to Me, and I will answer you, and show you great and mighty things, which you do not know" (NKJV). When you call out to God (i.e. pray), He will answer. That's a promise! When you pray, God gets to work. I love this saying, "When we work, we work; but when we pray, God works" (source unknown). When you pray, He releases His power. God will show you great and mighty things…*when* you pray. But you must take the initiative and pray.

I have often heard it said that Jeremiah 33:3 is God's telephone number. You might want to write it down. It is J-E-R-3-3-3. When you dial this number, you will never get a busy signal. He is always available and waiting to hear from you.

As a Christian, you never have to feel helpless and powerless. You need never say, "There's nothing I can do." There is always something you can do. You can pray. Just like Elijah. Just like Elisha. You can call out to God. You've got His number. It's J-E-R-3-3-3. The line is never busy. Why don't you give Him a call today?

Strengthen Your Faith

How did God answer the prayers of Elijah and Elisha?

Describe a time in your life when it was obvious that God answered your prayer.

What are some things that keep you from praying?

Start a prayer journal, which records your prayer requests and God's answers.

36

THE SOVEREIGNTY OF GOD

Some faced jeers and flogging, while still others were chained and put in prison. They were stoned; they were sawed in two; they were put to death by the sword. They went about in sheepskins and goatskins, destitute, persecuted and mistreated—the world was not worthy of them. They wandered in deserts and mountains, and in caves and holes in the ground.
(Hebrews 11:36-38)

The Bible says very clearly that on your journey of faith, you will experience both mountaintops and valleys. There will be times when you feel like you are on top of the world, and times when you feel like the world is on top of you.

The people mentioned above lived by faith. Yet they were jeered at, flogged, and imprisoned. Some were even put to death. They were persecuted and mistreated by the world, because of their faith.

I don't have the answers to human suffering and tragedy, but I know Who does. God knows all things. God is in control of all things. Because I believe that God knows all things and God controls all things, I no longer feel the need to have all the answers in life. I believe that God is good and loving and kind. I believe that He will always do what is best for His world, which He created.

God is sovereign. He created the world and everything in it. He has the right to do whatever He chooses with His creation. Psalm 24:1 says, "The earth is the LORD'S, and everything in it, the world, and all who live in it."

God has a plan and a purpose for this world. You may not understand it, but that is because you are not God. Your job is not to understand God. Your job is to trust God and please Him. By faith, acknowledge that God is sovereign and is in total control of His world.

The sovereignty of God reminds me that there are no accidents or coincidences in life. Everything that happens in this world happens because God orchestrated it, or God allowed it. I don't believe that God orchestrates all the evil in the world. I don't believe that God sits up in heaven deciding when and where He will send the next Tsunami or tornado. I don't believe God causes the pain and suffering that you have experienced in your life.

We live in a sin-filled world. Man made the choice to rebel against God in the garden, and since that time pain, evil, and suffering have been allowed in this world. I tell my children, life is not fair, but God is good. I find great comfort in knowing that even though bad things happen, God is still in control. It gives me assurance and hope to know that when I experience tough times, the God who loves me is the God who is in total control of my life and this world.

In His sovereign power, God will take all things, both good and bad, and use them for His glory. My wife makes the best cherry pies in the world. As she makes these pies, she follows a recipe. Some of these ingredients do not taste very good by themselves. But when she puts them all together, and heats them in the oven, out comes a beautiful cherry pie.

"And we know that in all things God works for the good of those who love him, who have been called according to his purpose" (Romans 8:28). This is a great promise to those who live by faith. When you live by faith, nothing can bring you down. You believe that all things, the good, the bad, and the ugly, will ultimately be used to bring glory to God. You know that the God who loves you is in control.

Whether you are presently on the mountaintop, or down in the valley, you can take comfort in knowing that God is sovereign. He loves you and is always with you on your journey of faith. Travel with me to the Book of Daniel for a real-life example of what God's sovereignty is all about.

Shadrach, Meshach, And Abednego In The Fiery Furnace (Daniel 3)

Shadrach, Meshach, and Abednego were three Jewish boys taken from Jerusalem into captivity by the Babylonians in 605 BC. Nebuchadnezzar was the king of Babylon. He made a golden image, which he required all people to worship. Anyone who failed to worship the golden image would be thrown into a blazing furnace.

Shadrach, Meshach, and Abednego were faithful to God and refused to worship the golden image. Their response, when brought before King Nebuchadnezzar, demonstrates their strong faith.

> If we are thrown into the blazing furnace, the God we serve is able to save us from it, and he will rescue us from your hand, O king. But even if he does not, we want you to know, O king, that we will not serve your gods or worship the image of gold you have set up. (Daniel 3:17-18)

The king was furious and ordered the furnace heated seven times hotter than usual. Shadrach, Meshach, and Abednego were tied up and thrown inside. The fire was so hot that it killed the soldiers who escorted them to the furnace. King Nebuchadnezzar noticed there were four men walking in the fire. The king let Shadrach, Meshach, and Abednego out of the furnace and realized they were unharmed. Their rope bindings were the only thing destroyed by the fire.

Shadrach, Meshach, And Abednego Lived By Faith

Shadrach, Meshach, and Abednego suffered tremendous heartache in their lifetime. They watched as Nebuchadnezzar conquered Jerusalem. They were carried off to a foreign land. Everything that was familiar vanished from their lives. They had to learn a new language and were even given new names. Shadrach, Meshach, and Abednego were indoctrinated with foreign customs and forced to serve a government, which was not their own (see Daniel 1).

Shadrach, Meshach, and Abednego lived by faith. They showed the depth of their faith when they were called before Nebuchadnezzar to explain their failure to bow down to the golden idol. Nebuchadnezzar said he would let them go if they worshiped the golden image. But if they failed to bow, they would be thrown into the fiery furnace.

Shadrach, Meshach, and Abednego refused to compromise their beliefs. They demonstrated amazing faith when they said they would stand for God, even if God chose not to deliver them from the fire (see Daniel 3:18). Nothing would cause them to turn away from their faith, not even impending death.

The Sovereignty Of God

Shadrach, Meshach, and Abednego correctly understood the sovereignty of God. It is false theology to say that God *must* deliver you because you have faith. It is correct to say He *may* deliver you, if deliverance is part of His sovereign purpose.

"Faith movement" theology teaches you can cause anything to happen if you have enough faith. This teaching is not backed up with Scripture. The Bible is filled with people who suffered for their faith. Elijah, Elisha, Nehemiah, Isaiah, Jeremiah, Micaiah, Hanani, and Zechariah, all alluded to in Hebrews 11:36-38, are only some of the faithful who were persecuted and mistreated by the world. Some of these faithful servants were even killed.

God Is With You

Faith did not keep Shadrach, Meshach, and Abednego from experiencing a terrifying situation. It was because of their faith that they were thrown into a fiery furnace. Some people think God took the heat out of the furnace. I do not believe that because the soldiers who took them to the furnace were burned to death at the door.

There was a fourth person in the fire with them. God enabled Shadrach, Meshach, and Abednego to walk around unharmed in the fire. T.D. Jakes said, "Real faith doesn't mean you won't go through the fire. Real faith simply means that when you pass through the fire, He will be with you."[1]

Faith does not keep you out of trouble. Quite the contrary, it can cause you tremendous trouble in this world. If you are not delivered from your troubles, it does not mean you lack faith. But by faith, you are able to handle an experience that others cannot.

When you find yourself in a difficult situation, lean on God. Remember, you are indwelled by the Holy Spirit. He is there with you in the fire. Allow the Spirit to comfort and strengthen you in hard times. "May the God of hope fill you with all joy and peace as you trust in him, so that you may overflow with hope by the power of the Holy Spirit" (Romans 15:13).

Strengthen Your Faith

How would you define the sovereignty of God?

How did Shadrach, Meshach, and Abednego acknowledge God's sovereignty?

What is the relationship between faith and the sovereignty of God?

In what area of your life do you need to be reminded that God is in control? Discuss this with Him today.

37

THE ARROWS OF AFFLICTION

Some faced jeers and flogging, while still others were chained and put in prison. They were stoned; they were sawed in two; they were put to death by the sword. They went about in sheepskins and goatskins, destitute, persecuted and mistreated—the world was not worthy of them. They wandered in deserts and mountains, and in caves and holes in the ground.
(Hebrews 11:36-38)

    A friend of mine, who is a bow hunter, once gave me an arrow to use for an illustration on pain. He told me that it is much more painful to be shot by an arrow than a bullet. I told him I would take his word for it, as I did not care to test his theory! My friend told me that once an arrow penetrates the flesh, the pain continues. The arrow cannot be pulled out of the body, like a bullet, because the ragged edges of the arrow will cause additional destruction. If you attempt to pull, turn, or twist the arrow, the pain will only increase. As I thought about the pain and torture that can be inflicted by an arrow, my mind turned to the many Christians who have been shot by an arrow of affliction.

    I'm not talking about the small problems of life. Those are darts. I'm talking about arrows. I'm talking about the family who spent their life savings to build their dream home, only to have it blown away in a hurricane. I'm talking about my friend, whose twenty-year-old daughter was killed, when a man fell asleep at the wheel, and ran head-on into her car. I'm talking about the parents who lost not one, but two daughters, to cancer in the last year. No, I'm not talking about darts. I'm talking about arrows, which are plunged deep into the body. I'm talking about pain and suffering; wounds that don't heal overnight.

The Bible is filled with stories of men and women who were struck by the arrow of affliction. Many of these, like the people mentioned above, suffered because of their faith. Why would God allow people of faith to experience these arrows of affliction? What is the purpose of suffering?

Metal Is Purified With Fire

I have learned in my own life that God uses suffering to draw me closer to Him. I also know people who have turned away from God during times of affliction. Adversity provides an opportunity to turn away from God, or draw near to Him. When you are in pain, you can choose to shake your fist at God and run away, or call out to Him for help.

You can probably remember a time when you gained wisdom through a painful experience. I believe that God allows these afflictions to mold you into the person He wants you to be. Through your trials, He purifies and reshapes you into His very own image. This process is very similar to the one used in refining precious metals.

After gold and silver is mined, it must be refined to purify the metal. The refining process separates pure metal from the impurities in the ore during the smelting process. A metal worker cannot make something beautiful until the impurities are taken away.

Fire is used to purify gold and silver. It requires a very high temperature to remove impurities. For example, silver does not melt until it reaches 1760.9 degrees Farenheit. When the correct temperature is reached the impurities are removed by skimming them off the top. A refiner will keep the heat turned on as long as it is needed.

The metal is purified when the refiner can clearly see his own reflection in the molten liquid. If his reflection is unclear, he must continue with the process. When he can see his face clearly, the refining process is complete.

God Uses Fiery Trials To Purify You

Just as fire is used to purify metal, God uses fire to purify you. He allows hardship into your life to purify your heart. Isaiah 1:25 says, "I will turn my hand against you; I will thoroughly purge away your dross and remove all your impurities."

Webster's defines dross as "scum formed on the surface of molten metal; waste matter; worthless stuff." God gets rid of the worthless stuff in your life through the fire of a test or a trial. God must take things out of your life that should not be there, to enable you to become the person He desires you to be.

Life in the twenty-first century is cluttered with worthless stuff. Materialism is prevalent in our culture. Everyone wants a bigger house, a pool in their yard, the latest electronic equipment, a new SUV, or a vacation to Australia. Most people, even Christians, spend more time acquiring "stuff" than they do with the Lord. God will intervene with fire if your life revolves around things, or you have to juggle the books to pay for them. He wants you to get your priorities straight.

Busyness clutters your life with activity. I hear this scenario all the time: You have three children. You work, volunteer at your child's school, and are the assistant coach of their soccer team. Your kids have karate lessons on Tuesday and piano lessons on Thursday. And do not forget about Cub Scouts on

Monday and Girl Scouts on Wednesday. The soccer team has games every Saturday morning. Sunday is your only day to sleep in, and so you often do not make it to church. Or maybe you come to church every Sunday, but consider yourself too busy to participate in a ministry of your church. If your life is too busy for God, a purge is inevitable. God wants to remove the activity (even if it is of noble purpose) that keeps you from spending time with Him.

Not only does God want to purge the dross from your life, He also wants to remove any impurities. Impurities are the immoral actions and sins in your life. The impurity may be an inappropriate relationship, or a negative thought pattern. It can be an attitude, or a bad habit. It may be a deliberate sin, or something you are not even aware is a problem for God. During a trial, God shows you what impurity needs to be taken out, what hinders your relationship.

God's Hand Is On The Thermostat

It requires a very high temperature to purify gold and silver. In the same way, God uses heat to remove spiritual impurities during the refining process. The heat of your trials may be very intense. The good news is that God has his hand on the thermostat. He knows how much heat is needed to accomplish His purpose in your life. It will not be more than you can bear.

A refiner knows his work is finished when he can clearly see his own reflection in the molten liquid. As He works, God looks to see if He can see His reflection in you. God refines you because He wants you to be conformed into the likeness of Jesus (see Romans 8:29). His ultimate goal is to make you like Christ (see 1 John 3:2). When He can see Himself clearly in you, God turns off the heat.

Years ago I saw a cartoon, which said, "Ain't nothing going

to happen to me today, that me and the Lord can't handle!" Isn't that the truth? You will go through fiery trials in life. That is a given. Some will be hotter than others. The promise of the Bible is that God has his hand on the thermostat. God will not allow any trial to come into your life that together you can't handle. God is in control of all things, even the arrows of affliction.

Trials Prove Your Faith To Be Genuine

I love this Scripture:

> In this you greatly rejoice, though now for a little while you may have had to suffer grief in all kinds of trials. These have come so that your faith—of greater worth than gold, which perishes even though refined by fire—may be proved genuine and may result in praise, glory and honor when Jesus Christ is revealed. (1 Peter 1:6-7)

On the journey of faith, you will experience arrows of affliction. It's not a question of whether you will experience trials, but rather how you will respond. Affliction can either turn you away from God or draw you near to Him. When you respond by faith in times of hardship, you demonstrate to the world that your faith is real.

God uses tough times to take away the impurities, which dull your character and faith. He knows the amount of heat, which is needed to purify and perfect your faith. When the refining is finished, you shine brilliantly. You reflect Christ and prove your faith to be genuine.

Strengthen Your Faith

Describe a trial in your life, which caused your faith to grow and mature.

According to James 1:2-3, how are you to respond to trials?

Reflect on the purification process of precious metals. Ask God to use the trials in your life to make you more like Him.

38

TURNING TRAGEDY INTO WORSHIP

> *Some faced jeers and flogging, while still others were chained and put in prison. They were stoned; they were sawed in two; they were put to death by the sword. They went about in sheepskins and goatskins, destitute, persecuted and mistreated—the world was not worthy of them. They wandered in deserts and mountains, and in caves and holes in the ground.*
> (Hebrews 11:36-38)

You may remember seeing a news story about a tragic train wreck outside of Los Angeles. A man who wanted to commit suicide parked his car on the railroad track. At the last minute, he changed his mind and fled his car. The train hit the car, derailed, and caused numerous deaths and injuries. Many innocent people were affected by this tragedy, which caused many to question how something like this could happen.

Dr. Henry Cloud says that everyone will experience a "train wreck" in life. It is unlikely that yours will be a literal train wreck. Instead, it will be a tragedy or adversity, which has severe implications.

There is probably nothing more confusing than when you see bad things happen to good people. You may hear the fairness of God questioned when a young father is killed serving his country. Maybe he was a strong Christian, very active in his church and now leaves behind a wife and three small children.

Or maybe you know a Christian couple that discovered their only child has cancer.

Sometimes life seems so unfair! You can't help but ask the question, "How can God let such bad things happen to such good people?" When you look at the verses above, I think it's clear this is not a new question. Even in the Old Testament, people of faith experienced unexplained tragedies and hardships.

Is it possible to worship God in the midst of trial and adversity? I believe it is. As I have matured in my faith, I find I no longer blame suffering and tragedy on God. Tragedy happens in life. Through it all, I find that God is good and worthy to be praised.

In Psalm 50:15 God says, "And call upon me in the day of trouble; I will deliver you, and you will honor me." That is my goal. In times of trouble, I want to honor God. In times of tragedy, I want to worship Him. Even when I experience a "train wreck" in life, I want others to see that my hope and my faith are firmly rooted in a sovereign God. Yes, bad things happen, but God is still worthy to be praised.

Job

The confusion associated with adversity and suffering is as old as time itself. Consider Job. When you think about bad things happening to good people, Job would have to be at the top of the list. The Book of Job is the oldest book in the Bible, predating the Ten Commandments and the Book of Genesis. It deals with the question all of humanity asks, "Why does God allow bad things to happen to good people?"

Job was from the land of Uz. He had a wife, seven sons and three daughters. Job was very wealthy, and considered the greatest man among the people of the East. He had seven thousand sheep, three thousand camels, five hundred yoke of oxen, and five hundred donkeys. Job was considered blameless and upright. He was a man who feared God and shunned evil (see Job 1:1-3).

One day, Satan told God that Job was only righteous because he was rich. God allowed Satan to test Job's faith. In one day, Job lost his children, servants and livestock. Only he and his wife survived. Job was devastated, but he did not blame God. He acknowledged everything belonged to God. Job praised God despite his misfortune (see Job 1:6-22).

Satan returned to God. He said Job would curse God if his body were damaged. Satan afflicted Job with painful sores all over his body. Job's wife encouraged him to curse God and he refused. Job was prepared to accept both blessing and adversity from God (see Job 2:1-10).

Sometimes the righteous suffer, and never know why. This was true in Job's case. But through his experiences he learned to trust God even when he did not understand. He trusted God with everything. Job encountered God through his ordeal and his faith soared to new levels. Job 42:5 says, "My ears have heard of you but now my eyes have seen you."

Job's faith enabled him to triumph over adversity. God gave him three daughters and seven sons. The Lord blessed the second part of Job's life more than the first. He became prosperous and was given twice what he had before. He died at an old age (see Job 42:10-17).

Job Chose To Worship In Adversity

In the blink of an eye, Job lost all of his children, his servants and his livestock. One minute, life was fantastic, and the next minute it was sheer agony. Satan was wrong about Job (a fact which God knew all along). His faith was not determined by circumstances. Job loved God and lived by faith when he had everything and when he had nothing. Job held to his faith, even though he never understood the reason for his suffering. He shows authentic faith is possible in the most difficult of circumstances.

Job's reaction to overwhelming loss is amazing. When Job lost everything, his immediate reaction was to worship (see Job 1:20). Job praised God despite his misfortune (see Job 1:21). He realized that God alone is sovereign (see Job 1:21).

The most intimate worship occurs when you praise God during suffering. This only happens when you realize that praising the Lord has nothing to do with the circumstances of your life. Worship has everything to do with who God is. Your faith in God is constant because He never changes (see Hebrews 13:8).

<u>Job Lived By Faith Because He Placed His Hope In God</u>

Job placed his hope in God (see Job 13:15). By definition, faith is being sure of what you hope for (see Hebrews 11:1). Job placed his hope in God because he trusted him. He trusted God because he knew Him. Job went from hearing of God to seeing Him (see Job 42:5).

When you trust God by faith during adversity, you become strong. When you worship in your darkest hour, God is there to hold you up and strengthen you. When you find yourself in a hopeless situation (like Job), realize that God is hope.

Hebrews 11:36-38 clearly shows that a faithful servant of God can expect to experience both mental and physical suffering during their lifetime. Strong faith enables you to deal with both mental and physical anguish. The next time you find yourself in pain or tragedy, consider the faith of God's servant Job. Follow his example and turn your tragedy into worship.

Displaying God's Glory

Your pain has a purpose. No one ever said that the journey of faith was easy. It may be filled with heartache and trouble. Yet tragedy often serves as an opportunity to give glory and honor to God. When you worship God in the tough times, others see God in you.

Think of your life as a frame, which displays the glory of God. God can use whatever He chooses to display His glory: the natural wonders of the world, the birth of a newborn baby, or people who worship Him during tragedy. All the people mentioned in Hebrews 11 worshiped God in the midst of personal tragedy. They displayed the glory of God when they chose to live by faith during their suffering.

Everyone will experience a train wreck in life. You are not exempt. As a follower of Christ, you will know times of personal heartache. Learn from Job's example: turn your tragedy into worship. Instead of complaining about your problems, use them to display the glory of God in your life.

Strengthen Your Faith

Describe a train wreck you have experienced. How did it affect your faith?

How can the story of Job encourage you during times of tragedy?

What purpose might God have for your pain and suffering?

Praise has nothing to do with your circumstances. It has everything to do with who God is. Meditate on this thought as you worship God today.

39

DELAYED REWARDS

These were all commended for their faith, yet none of them received what had been promised.
(Hebrews 11:39)

Abraham Lincoln desired to make a difference as a public servant. However, his road to success was not an easy one. At the age of 22, he failed in business. When Lincoln was 23, he ran for the Legislature, and lost. At the age of 24, he again failed in business. When Lincoln was 25, he was elected to the Legislature. When he was 26, his fiancée died. He had a nervous breakdown when he was 27. At age 28, Lincoln failed to be elected Speaker, and when he was 31, he lost his race for Elector.

Lincoln was defeated when he ran for Congress at age 34. At the age of 39, he ran for Congress a second time. He lost that election as well. When he was 46, he lost his bid for a Senate seat, and at 47, he failed to be elected Vice President. Lincoln ran for the Senate a second time, at age 49, and was defeated.

At the age of 51, Abraham Lincoln was elected President of the United States of America. Although he experienced many delays along the way, he stayed true to his calling, and God recorded every act of faithful service in His book of remembrance. I believe God used the years that Lincoln lived in obscurity and failure to mold and shape him into the man who would abolish slavery in this country. Abraham Lincoln served faithfully, and in God's timing, he became one of the greatest presidents in the history of our nation.

God gives His best to those who wait on Him. The world wants instant gratification, but I believe the best things in life take time, often much longer than you ever expected. I call them delayed rewards, because many times they come after months or even years of dedicated service. This was true in the life of Abraham Lincoln, and it is true in your life as well. When you live by faith, and wait patiently on God, you will receive His best.

Mordecai Saved The King's Life

There are many stories in the Bible about delayed rewards. My personal favorite is about a man named Mordecai, a wise and courageous leader in the Old Testament. His story is found in the Book of Esther. Mordecai lived in Susa, the capital city of Persia, during the reign of King Xerxes. Mordecai was the older cousin of Queen Esther. When Esther's parents died, Mordecai adopted Esther and raised her as his own (see Esther 2:7). Because of his close relationship to the queen, Mordecai was given a privileged seat at the king's gate. The king's gate was the place where official business was transacted.

One day, when Mordecai was sitting at the king's gate, he overheard two of the king's officers plotting to assassinate King Xerxes. Mordecai told Esther about the conspiracy, and she reported it to the king, giving credit to Mordecai. An investigation proved the information to be accurate, and the two guards were hanged. Details of the conspiracy, including Mordecai's role in uncovering the plot, were recorded in the book of the annals (see Esther 2:19-23).

Mordecai's Reward Was Delayed (Esther 6:1-11)

One night, five years later, the king could not sleep. Xerxes ordered his servant to read aloud from the book of the chronicles, the official record of his reign. (There is nothing like a history book to cure insomnia!) Providentially, the volume that detailed Mordecai's role in uncovering the assassination plot was chosen.

When the servant finished reading, the king asked if Mordecai had been rewarded for saving his life. The servant told the king Mordecai had received nothing. King Xerxes ordered that Mordecai be honored in a very public way: Mordecai was dressed in a royal robe and placed on the king's horse. The king's second in command led him through the city streets, proclaiming, "This is what is done for the man the king delights to honor!" (Esther 6:11b). Mordecai was finally honored, in a very public way, for his good deed.

Five years passed between when Mordecai saved the king's life and when he received his reward. It appeared as though Mordecai's good deed was all but forgotten. But God made sure that didn't happen. He saw to it that the event was permanently recorded in an official book. When the time was right, the book was opened, the king remembered, and Mordecai received his reward.

God Keeps A Book Of Remembrance

Ancient kings kept books of remembrance, which recorded peoples' names and the special deeds they performed. In the same way, God records and remembers the deeds of His children. The Bible teaches that God keeps a detailed record of those who fear and honor Him.

> Then those who feared the LORD talked with each other, and the LORD listened and heard. A scroll of remembrance was written in his presence concerning those who feared the LORD and honored his name. "They will be mine," says the LORD Almighty, "in the day when I make up my treasured possession. I will spare them, just as in compassion a man spares his son who serves him. And you will again see the distinction between the righteous and the wicked, between those who serve God and those who do not." (Malachi 3:16-18)

The book of remembrance provides a detailed history of your life. God is watching what you do and is recording it in His book. And He doesn't just document the highlights. Every event is recorded—every thought, every word, every action. He has a complete dossier on you.

Think of the book of remembrance as your permanent record. And when I say permanent, I mean permanent. It will follow you all the way into eternity. The actual reward you receive in heaven is dependent upon the deeds you perform here on earth. In other words, the value of the deeds recorded in the book of remembrance will be used to determine your reward in heaven.

Delayed Rewards

The faithful of Hebrews 11 have been dead for a long time. However, they have not yet been rewarded for their faithful service during their life on earth. For example, Abraham lived approximately 2000 BC. That means he has been dead 4,000 years, and he still hasn't been rewarded.

It may seem to you that God is taking an awfully long time

to reward His faithful servants. You need to understand that God does not work according to your timetable. God is eternal. He is beyond time. 2 Peter 3:8 says, "With the Lord a day is like a thousand years, and a thousand years are like a day." Psalm 90:4 says, "For a thousand years in your sight are like a day that has just gone by, or like a watch in the night." When you put it that way, Abraham hasn't been waiting 4,000 years for his reward; he has only waited four days!

God, in His sovereignty, has decided to unfold His plan for mankind across an expanse of time. But why does His plan have to take so long? The Bible provides the answer to this question in 2 Peter 3:9: "The Lord is not slow in keeping his promise, as some understand slowness. He is patient with you, not wanting anyone to perish, but everyone to come to repentance." Our loving God does not want anyone to end up in hell. He wants everyone to profess faith in Jesus Christ and accept the grace He so freely gives.

<u>The Faithful Will Be Rewarded</u>

At the appointed time, God will open the book of remembrance and judge the works of every believer. Those who were faithful will receive their reward. My prayer is that you will take to heart this truth: *what you do in your mortal lifetime has a direct correlation to what you will do for all eternity.*

Commit your life to God. Live for His purposes and His glory. *If you choose to live by faith, one day you will be rewarded.* And what a blessing it will be to hear the words, "Well done, good and faithful servant!" (see Matthew 25:21).

Strengthen Your Faith

Describe a time in your life when you received a delayed reward. How did you feel during the delay?

Isaiah 40:31 says, "But those who *wait* on the LORD shall renew their strength; they shall mount up with wings like eagles, they shall run and not be weary, they shall walk and not faint" (NKJV, emphasis added). According to this verse, what are the benefits of waiting on the Lord?

Read 1 Corinthians 15:58. What does this verse teach about delayed rewards?

Read Hebrews 11:6. What does God do for those who earnestly seek Him?

40

PERFECT PEOPLE IN A PERFECT PLACE

God had planned something better for us so that only together with us would they be made perfect.
(Hebrews 11:40)

As we come to the end of our forty-day journey of faith, I trust that you have gained a better understanding of what it means to live by faith. You have learned that the journey of faith includes both triumphs and trials. You will experience times of joy and sorrow, and learn many lessons along the way. But where does the journey end? It ends in a perfect place called heaven, which is your eternal home. One day, you will live in a perfect body in a perfect world with a perfect God. At the end of your journey of faith you will live forever in a state of perfection.

As an accounting major in college, one of the first things I learned was that a product has three stages. The first stage of a product is the raw materials. The second stage is called work in process. The final stage is finished goods. There are also three stages in the Christian life. The first stage is justification. The second stage is sanctification, and the third is glorification.

Justification occurs when you trust Jesus Christ as your Lord and Savior. At the moment of salvation, you are justified, or declared right with God. Your name is written in the Lamb's Book of Life, and you begin the journey of faith.

Sanctification is what happens to you along your journey of faith. It is the work in process stage of the Christian life. Sanctification means "to be set apart." As a believer, you have been set apart for God and set apart from sin. As your faith grows and matures, you become conformed to the likeness of Jesus Christ (see Romans 8:29). In other words, you become more and more like Jesus—you live your life for God and His purposes, not for yourself. This happens through a process called discipleship, whereby God uses prayer, study, trials, circumstances, and relationships to mold you and make you into the person He wants you to be.

Glorification is what happens to you when you enter the realm of eternity. When you die, your soul and spirit leave your body and enter heaven, which is currently in the spiritual realm. For a Christian, to be absent from the body is to be at home with the Lord (see 2 Corinthians 5:8). You will be in the presence of Jesus and live in a sin-free environment. Eventually, every believer will receive a resurrected, glorified body, and heaven will be relocated to the new earth. On the new earth, you will have a perfect body, and live in a perfect place with a perfect God for all eternity. This place of perfection is the final destination on your journey of faith.

All Believers (Old & New Covenant) Will Be Made Perfect Together

The Bible teaches that, in the future, three things will happen to all believers: your body will be resurrected, you will stand before the judgment seat of Christ to receive your reward, and you will live for eternity with God on the new earth. In His sovereignty, God has decided all believers (from the old and the new covenant) will be made perfect together.

Heaven's Location Change

Most people view heaven as changeless. They think heaven will always be located in the spiritual realm, completely separated from the earthly realm. They visualize themselves floating on a cloud and playing the harp for all eternity. This is not the way heaven is described in Scripture.

Ezekiel said the name of heaven is, "The LORD is there" (see Ezekiel 48:35). To be in heaven is to be in the presence of God. In other words, heaven is where God lives. It is not where He must live. Heaven is where He chooses to live.

You learned in the lesson on Hebrews 11:3 that only God is self-existent. Everything else was created, including heaven. God alone is changeless (see Hebrews 13:8). Because heaven was created, it can change.

God currently lives in the spiritual realm, which is sometimes referred to as the intermediate heaven. This is where the soul and spirit of a believer goes when they die. However, this is *not* the final destination on the journey of faith.

In the future, the location of heaven will change. At the culmination of history, when the times have reached their fulfillment, all things on heaven and earth will be brought together under Jesus (see Ephesians 1:10). No longer will there be any separation between heaven and earth. The earthly realm and the spiritual realm will become one and the same. This future heaven will occur on the new earth. *The new earth is where you will spend eternity with God.*

Description Of The New Earth—Eternal Heaven

> Then I saw a new heaven and a new earth, for the first heaven and the first earth had passed away, and there was no longer any sea. I saw the Holy City, the new Jerusalem, coming down out of heaven from

God, prepared as a bride beautifully dressed for her husband. And I heard a loud voice from the throne saying, "Now the dwelling of God is with men, and he will live with them. They will be his people, and God himself will be with them and be their God. He will wipe away every tear from their eyes. There will be no more death or mourning or crying or pain, for the old order of things has passed away." (Revelation 21:1-4)

The Bible teaches that eternity in heaven will occur on the new earth. One day, the earth will be restored and transformed into the new earth. At that time, God will dwell with man on the earth. Because heaven is where God lives, heaven and the new earth become synonymous.

There are differing interpretations as to when the old earth will end and the new earth will begin. You may never know which view is correct until it actually happens. But make no mistake, it will happen. There will be a new earth, and it will be your final home.

The old earth began as a perfect place in the garden of Eden. It was changed because of the "curse" of sin. In the future, the earth will again be transformed into a perfect place. It will still be earth, but it will be changed and improved beyond your imagination. The new earth is made to endure and be your home for eternity (see Isaiah 66:22). The new earth will be a perfect place, where people of faith live in the presence of God.

You will live and work on the new earth in a resurrected body. Your new, resurrected body will resemble your old body. After all, you are the same person. You have just been changed. Jesus received the first resurrected body, and it was glorious. In His resurrected state, Jesus' body was both physical and recognizable (see Luke 24:36-43). Your body will be transformed into something glorious to enable you to live and work on the new earth. Because you will live on the new earth forever, your resurrected body must be imperishable (see 1 Corinthians 15:52-54).

Your Role On The New Earth

The new earth will be God's kingdom. It is where His original plan for mankind will be fulfilled. You may recall that in the beginning God gave mankind the task of ruling over creation (see Genesis 1:26-28). However, when sin entered the garden, God took rule of the earth away from man and gave it to Satan (see Ephesians 2:2)...temporarily. On the new earth, God will restore man to his intended place of authority over creation and man will assist Jesus with the administration of the new earth.

God and Jesus both work (see John 5:17), and so will you when you get to heaven. You will rule with Christ over creation forever (see Revelation 22:5). There will be a hierarchy of sorts on the new earth. Your position in the kingdom will be determined by the reward you receive at the judgment. Your reward is based on your faithfulness to God during your time on the old earth. (Read Luke 19:11-26 for further insight.)

God rewards His faithful children with increased responsibilities (i.e. work). You may be thinking, "That's just great. I was looking forward to an eternal vacation." The good news is that work on the new earth is not something you will have to endure, like so many people do today, living for the weekend or for the day they are finally able to retire. Quite the opposite will be true.

Increased service is a blessing, not a punishment. Remember, everything is perfect on the new earth. You will be working in a perfect environment, using your perfect body and your perfect mind to serve a perfect God. You will receive tremendous joy and experience an overwhelming sense of accomplishment in all that you do for the Lord.

Long For Heaven

Please realize that what you do in your mortal lifetime has a direct correlation to what you will do for all eternity. People with strong faith recognize this fact and reorganize their life according to God's will and agenda. You may remember the dot and line illustration used in the lesson on Hebrews 11:10.

•━━━━━━━━━━━━━━━━━━━━━━━━━━━▶

You currently live *in* the dot, but you should live *for* the line. That's what the journey of faith is all about. It is living for eternity while you are here on earth. Randy Alcorn calls this "living in light of eternity." People of great faith live their entire lives with eternity in mind because they literally long for heaven (see Hebrews 11:16).

As this forty-day study comes to a close, I pray you will take what you have learned and apply it to your own journey of faith. Develop a longing for heaven. When you purposely set your heart on heaven, you will look forward to it. The more you look toward heaven, the more you will find yourself wanting it. And before you know it, you will long for heaven, just like the heroes of Hebrews 11.

I pray God has spoken to you during this forty-day journey. As I said in the introduction, my goal is to help you develop and strengthen your faith. In the past forty days, you have learned that faith is indeed like a roller coaster. It is a ride of ups and downs, twists and turns, with complete assurance that you will arrive at your ultimate destination. Once you arrive, you will see that you are a perfect person in a perfect place.

As you get off the ride, you will see people like Noah, Abraham, and Isaac. You will see Jacob, Joseph, and Moses. You will find yourself surrounded by David, Samuel, and all the prophets of God. But the first person you will see is the one you have longed to see since the day you began your journey. You will look directly into the eyes of Jesus. As you arrive at your ultimate destination and reflect on your journey of faith, my prayer is that you will be able to say, "What a ride! What an awesome ride!"

Strengthen Your Faith

What is the first thing that comes to mind when you think about heaven?

The three stages of the Christian life are justification, sanctification, and glorification. Write a brief description of each term.

Describe how your Christian life is a "work in process." In what ways have you matured during the past forty days?

Make a list of the people in Hebrews 11 that inspired you. Allow them to motivate you as you continue on your journey of faith.

CONCLUSION

It all begins with faith. That has been the theme of our journey over the past forty days. As we conclude our study time together, I want to reiterate that you can receive eternal life in heaven and an abundant life here on earth. All you need to do is enter into a personal relationship with Jesus Christ.

A friend once told me an acronym for faith, which I have never forgotten: **F**orsaking **A**ll **I** **T**rust **H**im. **FAITH**. It really is that simple. You are saved by faith alone.

If you desire to receive God's gift of eternal life, you can do so right now. Simply pray from your heart:

Dear Jesus,

I want to live a life of faith. Today, I forsake all and trust my life to You. I accept that you are God's Son, and believe that You died on the cross to pay the price for my sins. By faith, I receive Your forgiveness today and commit my life to You. Thank you, Jesus, for saving me and giving me the gift of eternal life. From this day forward, I pledge to live my life by faith.

In Jesus' name I pray,

Amen.

ENDNOTES

Chapter 1

1. Jim Cymbala with Dean Merrill, *Fresh Faith* (Grand Rapids, Mich.: Zondervan, 1999), 199-200.
2. *Life Application Study Bible (NIV)* (Wheaton, IL: Tyndale House Publishers, 1988), 2463.
3. Tony Evans, *Life Essentials* (Chicago, IL: Moody Publishers, 2003), 96.

Chapter 2

1. *Life Application Study Bible (NIV)* (Wheaton, IL: Tyndale House Publishers, 1988), 2482.

Chapter 6

1. W.E. Vine, *Vine's Concise Dictionary of Bible Words* (Nashville, TN: Thomas Nelson, 1999), 334-335.

Chapter 7

1. Ronald F. Youngblood, F.F. Bruce and R.K. Harrison, *Nelson's New Illustrated Bible Dictionary* (Nashville, TN: Thomas Nelson, 1995), 908.

Chapter 8

1. *Life Application Study Bible (NIV)* (Wheaton, IL: Tyndale House Publishers, 1988), 26.

Chapter 10

1. Ronald F. Youngblood, F.F. Bruce and R.K. Harrison, *Nelson's New Illustrated Bible Dictionary* (Nashville, TN: Thomas Nelson, 1995), 1281.
2. Bruce Wilkinson with David Kopp, *A Life God Rewards* (Sisters, OR: Multnomah Publishers, 2002), 19.

Chapter 13

1. Jim Cymbala, *Breakthrough Prayer* (Grand Rapids, Mich.: Zondervan, 2003), 118.

Chapter 14

1. Greg Ogden, *Transforming Discipleship* (Downers Grove, IL: InterVarsity Press, 2003), 33.

Chapter 17

1. Bruce Wilkinson, *Secrets of the Vine* (Sisters, OR: Multnomah Publishers, 2001), 73.

Chapter 18

1. *Life Application Study Bible (NIV)* (Wheaton, IL: Tyndale House Publishers, 1988), 2495.

Chapter 19

1. *Life Application Study Bible (NIV)* (Wheaton, IL: Tyndale House Publishers, 1988), 2474.

Chapter 25

1. Tony Evans, *Life Essentials* (Chicago, IL: Moody Publishers, 2003), 70-71.
2. Ibid., 71.

Chapter 31

1. Ronald F. Youngblood, F.F. Bruce and R.K. Harrison, *Nelson's New Illustrated Bible Dictionary* (Nashville, TN: Thomas Nelson, 1995), 1077-1078.

Chapter 34

1. Gayle D. Erwin, "Memorandum" *Servant Quarters: servant.org* (March 21, 2005).

Chapter 35

1. Jack Hayford, *Prayer Is Invading the Impossible* (Gainesville, FL: Bridge-Logos Publishers, 2002), 80.

Chapter 36

1. T.D. Jakes, *Can You Stand to be Blessed?* (Shippensburg, PA: Treasure House, 1994), 40.